IN OUR
BROKENNESS,
HE IS STRONG

IN OUR
BROKENNESS,
HE IS STRONG

TERESA COSTOUROS

XULON PRESS

Xulon Press
2301 Lucien Way #415
Maitland, FL 32751
407.339.4217
www.xulonpress.com

Unless otherwise indicated, Scripture quotations taken from the Holy Bible,
New Living Translation (NLT). Copyright ©1996, 2004, 2007 by Tyndale House
Foundation. Used by permission of Tyndale House Publishers, Inc.

Printed in the United States of America.
Edited by Xulon Press.

ISBN-13: 9781545623954

DEDICATION

To my precious son, Jason, without whose permission this book could not have been written. I also dedicate this book to my husband John and daughter Joanna, who share in the heartbreak and grief journey of our story.

ACKNOWLEDGMENTS

I would like to acknowledge and thank all the people who helped edit my manuscript and gave me feedback on content: my husband, John, and daughter, Joanna. Marilyn, your editing skills improved the clarity of my story.

I would also like to thank Pastor Keith Taylor, Angie LaFavor, and Dave Spooner for reviewing my manuscript and endorsing this book.

Last, but not least, I would like to thank Xulon Press. In partnership with the team at Xulon, I feel like together we are joining in what God is doing. Your advice and support has made this book possible.

"Don't be afraid, for I am with you.
Do not be dismayed, for I am your God.
I will strengthen you. I will help you.
I will uphold you with my victorious
right hand.

—Isaiah 41:10

I am holding you by your right hand—I, the
Lord your God.
And I say to you, 'Do not be afraid, I am
here to help you.'"

—Isaiah 41:13

TABLE OF CONTENTS

Prologue xiii
Chapter 1   A Mother's Worst Nightmare 1
Chapter 2   Where Are You, God? 5
Chapter 3   The Gift of Salvation 9
Chapter 4   God Answers Prayer 13
Chapter 5   A Life of Crime Begins 23
Chapter 6   Sentencing and Prison Time 31
Chapter 7   Here We Go Again 41
Chapter 8   The Transition 49
Chapter 9   The Halfway House 61
Chapter 10   Second Chances 65
Chapter 11   Forgiveness and Love 75
Chapter 12   And Then There Were Three 79
Chapter 13   Life after Death 85
Chapter 14   Working Things for Good 89

PROLOGUE

W hether or not we are God's children, we all walk through life and undergo many struggles and hardships. When it rains, it rains on all of us. The difference for Christians is that we have God to guide and counsel us. "You will keep on guiding me with your counsel, leading me to a glorious destiny" (Ps. 73:24). We find hope in God when everything looks hopeless. He walks at our side and keeps our hands in His. His word is a light unto our path.

If you have accepted Jesus as your Lord and Savior, it is my hope that this book will encourage and bless you as you continue your walk with God. It is also my desire that it will help you appreciate life's struggles and help you remember to place your complete faith in Jesus.

> Dear brothers and sisters, whenever trouble comes your way, let it be an opportunity for joy. For when your faith is tested, your endurance has a chance to grow. So let it grow, for when your endurance is fully developed, you will be strong in character and ready for anything (James 1:2–4).

Praise God for the opportunity to be renewed and strengthened and for His faithfulness, which is not conditional on our faithfulness. In our darkest hour, we may feel God has left us. Don't rely on feelings, but on His promises. His word is true "And be sure of this: I am with you always, even to the end of the age" (Matt. 28:20b).

If you do not know Jesus Christ, I pray that God will be revealed to you through my story and will stir a longing within your heart to know Him personally. I pray that you will search for the truth and that you will find God—the one and only God. There is no other; there is none like Him. God never goes back on His promise, and His word tells us "if you look for me in earnest, you will find me when you seek me" (Jer. 29:13).

CHAPTER 1

A MOTHER'S WORST NIGHTMARE

O n a cold Saturday evening in February of 2007, I peered out the window of the aircraft I was in at the snow covering the ground. We were landing at the airport in Edmonton, Alberta. I felt cold just seeing the snow. I was returning home after spending a fabulous week in sunny Guadalajara, Mexico.

The week spent in Guadalajara was so much fun. I was there with some colleagues on a study tour. It had been an amazing week, filled with many cultural and historical activities, enjoyment of a variety of Mexican cuisine, and of course, shopping. Anyone who knows me even just a little, quickly realizes that in addition to my love for God and my family, I have a tremendous passion for travel, fine dining, and shopping. What can be better than combining it all together? I couldn't wait to tell my husband, son, and daughter about my adventure. Both of my children were young adults in their early twenties at that time. My daughter, Joanna, lived on her own. My son, Jason, was living with my husband, John, and me.

I was scheduled to arrive home around ten o'clock in the evening. John had agreed to pick me up at the airport, and I thought it was quite likely that Jason and Joanna might accompany him. It would be great to see them all and enjoy some warm, fuzzy family stuff. Although I had only been gone for a week and was enjoying myself immensely, not a day had gone by that I didn't think of my family.

Upon my arrival in Phoenix, Arizona, I found out that my connecting flight to Edmonton had been delayed for a couple of hours. I didn't want John to go to the airport and have to wait for my flight, so I called him to let him know I wouldn't be arriving until midnight. When he answered the telephone, I immediately sensed in his voice that something was wrong. Because there had been a past history of some difficulties with Jason, I asked if everything was OK with Jason specifically. John replied, "Don't worry. Everything is OK. We'll talk when you arrive." I knew he was holding out on me.

During the final flight from Phoenix, my mind began speculating on all that might be wrong. Had Jason quit his new job? Had he been fired? Did he get in a fight with someone? Did he and his father fight? Was he hurt or sick? Was he in an accident? Did he get high on drugs or alcohol? I knew something was wrong, and I knew it had to do with Jason. Never in my wildest dreams was I ready for the new reality I was about to face.

Upon arrival at the airport, I was met by John and Joanna. My sister, Carole, and her husband, Harry, were also there, as they had just arrived from a vacation in Puerto Vallarta, Mexico. Jason was not with John and Joanna, and I remember feeling disappointed. I knew he would be looking forward to seeing me, as we were very close. John looked very distressed, and Joanna was visibly upset.

I asked where Jason was, and John, looking uncomfortable, said he wasn't able to come. I wanted to dig deeper but decided to wait until we were alone. John probably didn't want to discuss the troubles in front of others. We chatted briefly with Carole and Harry while waiting to collect my luggage. We collected my baggage, and Carole and Harry left. When we were together in the car, I once again asked what was wrong.

John tried to gently broach the subject, while Joanna plunged right in. She exclaimed, "Mom, Jason isn't here because he was arrested. He was picked up by the police in a downtown apartment suite. He was with three friends, and there was a dead body in the apartment." Those horrific words kept resounding in my brain: dead body, dead body, dead body. I could not possibly comprehend what I was being told. This cannot be real. I must be in the midst of a nightmare—a really bad nightmare.

I remember screaming inside my head, "This cannot be happening, God. Please remove this cruel picture that my mind has conjured up." Joanna needed to release the horror story from her mind. Wide-eyed, she continued, "Someone living in the suite below called the police, and they all got arrested. The police are trying to charge them with murder. Dad and I have been so upset. We can't believe that Jason could have been a part of this horrific crime. I am so scared for my brother. I love him so much."

As more of the story unfolded, my devastation elevated. How can this possibly be true? It sounded like the kind of story that comes straight from a murder mystery. Even reading this type of fictional story would have left me feeling unsettled. How can I possibly get used to this new reality in my life?

John had not contacted me in Mexico because he didn't want to upset me or spoil my trip. He didn't want me to receive such shocking news while I was alone in a foreign country with no one to turn to. He knew there was nothing I would be able to do from there. No wonder he was so pale and emotionally drained. I cried and begged God for this not to be true. But it was!

The next day was Sunday. John, Joanna, and I were together at our home. I spent most of the day crying and trying to come to terms with the new reality I had to face. I had not slept a wink since leaving Mexico, so I tried to sleep a little in the afternoon. Family members were dropping by to offer their support. I prayed that God would give me the strength to carry on; I didn't know how I could. Although I knew the verse "Give all your worries and cares to God, for he cares about what happens to you" (1 Pet. 5:7), I felt that God was very far away from me, and I didn't even know how to pray at this time.

Once I was rested, I felt a strong need to know more about the details. I read the newspaper articles that had been published. I read them over and over again, trying to comprehend every detail. Other than what was reported in the paper, we had no additional information. John had not been able to speak to Jason by telephone, nor had he been given an opportunity to see him in person. Jason's lawyer had advised him that he was being held in the Remand Centre. We booked a visit with Jason for the earliest opportunity — Tuesday evening. I needed to see my son!

CHAPTER 2

WHERE ARE YOU GOD?

I returned to work on Monday. On the outside, it appeared that all was normal in my world. I know that God was at my side, giving me the strength to carry on. I focused on His word, which tells us, "I command you—be strong and courageous! Do not be afraid or discouraged. For the Lord your God is with you wherever you go" (Josh. 1:9).

How I got through that first day back to work while my life was torn apart is truly a miracle. I put one foot in front of the other, carrying on, patiently waiting for Tuesday evening when John, Joanna, and I could visit Jason. The moment finally arrived. After going through rigorous security, we were allowed to see him. We were on one side of a glass pane; Jason was on the other side. A telephone was the allowable mode of communication. He looked terrible in his prison garb.

We cried together as a family. How could this be happening to us? Jason assured us he was an innocent man who had been in the wrong place at the wrong time, but his lawyer had advised him not to discuss the alleged crime with anyone. We told him we didn't need to know the details; we believed in him and loved him deeply. Our role was not to judge or speculate but to love and support him. Our love is unconditional.

Life for me had never been so difficult. John and Joanna were both struggling as well. In addition to supporting Jason, we were all trying to support each other. Stick together as a family through thick and thin! Isn't that what we are supposed to do?

Silently, I struggled with many questions. Where are you God? Why can't I feel your presence? Your word promises, "I will be your God throughout your lifetime—until your hair is white with age. I made you and I will care for you. I will carry you along and save you" (Isa. 46:4). Why don't you hear my prayers? Don't you care about me? Don't you care about my family? You may know the number of hairs I have on my head, but why can't I find you when I really need you? Where are your peace, comfort, and mercy? All I feel is anger and betrayal. My wounded heart became hard and bitter. If this is how God's children have to live, who needs it? It seemed He had abandoned me in my darkest hour.

I had never felt so far from God and certainly not so angry. It also wasn't just this one isolated event that "pushed me over the edge" so to speak. This was just one of the bigger events, and I felt it was so insurmountable. In addition to the question "Why, God?" I questioned how He could allow this to happen to me and what possible good could come from it. I had always believed that He would not give me something that was too big for me to handle; well, this time He had. I decided that although I knew there was a God and although He truly did have the whole world in His hands, He probably didn't really care what happened in our day-to-day lives, and there was no point looking to Him for peace and comfort or help in this situation.

With this new way of thinking, I quit praying, reading God's word, and going to church. This was the beginning of a long season of unanswered questions for me. Very soon, I felt even further away from God. Looking back to those dark days, I reflect on the verse "Draw close to God and God will draw close to you" (James 4:8a). I felt unable to draw close to God under the circumstances. I was broken and miserable.

I tried to remember God's presence in difficult situations in the past, but I didn't want to think about any of it. I tried occasionally to pray, but I was unable. I did not know what to say in my misery. I knew that I had many Christian friends and family who were praying on my behalf, and although I was extremely grateful, that would have to be enough. I knew that John was praying, although his faith was also shaken.

The next year was filled with much sadness, anger, and apprehension. Although it appeared I was "handling" things on the outside, on the inside I was devastated. Jason was soon moved to a maximum-security penitentiary, while he awaited his trial. When the alleged crime was committed, he had been out on parole for a previous crime, so the parole was revoked, and he had to finish the remainder of the twenty-month sentence. We began our new routine in life, visiting our son once a week behind bars. Some prison staff were unkind and disrespectful to the families of inmates. That only added to our burden. Each time we visited, we underwent a rigorous search process. Sometimes the process even involved using drug-search dogs. Being fearful of dogs didn't matter; if I wanted to visit Jason, I had to ignore my fear and undergo the process. One time, I actually set off the drug scanner for heroin. I was shocked. I am so opposed to drugs. I just couldn't believe it. John made a joke about it, saying, "My wife is having a heroin experience." He thought it was bizarre that I, of all people, had set off the scanner. He knew I was completely anti-drug of any type. The guards, who had gotten to know us a little by then, were fair in this situation. After a few questions, they allowed me to proceed with the visit. It didn't impede future visits, either. What a relief!

I learned many other things about our justice system. It became clear that *rehabilitation* was much less of an objective than *punishment*. The prison was in "lock down" more often than one would expect. Visits were frequently suspended for lengthy periods of time. Again—anger! How can we support our loved one and keep him connected to the community, when all we have are sporadic telephone calls? I wrote letters to government politicians, federal cabinet ministers, and the prison warden, all to no avail. No one seemed to care. These inmates were the forgotten "dregs" of society! To use my son's own words, they were the "throwaways." Did God think they were worthy and able to be transformed through His power and grace?

Oh, God, where are you? It didn't seem that long ago that my family had placed our trust in the Lord. We had all accepted the gift of salvation and had become children of God. So, where was He through this storm? Why had He forgotten us? How could things have gotten *this* bad *this* quickly?

CHAPTER 3

THE GIFT OF SALVATION

❖

To understand the questions that arose in the midst of this turmoil, let me take you back in time. I had grown up in a family with a Christian mother and had attended Sunday school on a fairly regular basis as a child. I remember accepting Christ as my Savior as a young girl and the great awe and love I felt for God. He was definitely a significant aspect of my life, and I loved learning all the Bible stories and memorizing verses.

As a teenager, I learned it wasn't easy to be a Christian. How could one be "cool" and be a Christian? I soon began drifting away from God, and although I still believed, prayed on occasion (especially when I got into trouble and needed help), and periodically thought about God, I certainly was not in a close personal relationship with Him. Just before turning twenty years old, I met my husband-to-be, John. John was a new immigrant to Canada from Greece. He was Greek Orthodox and a university student, studying political science. We soon became inseparable and were married a few years later.

Throughout the early years of our marriage, we lived in several different cities in Canada. It was interesting to note that no matter where we moved, God continually sent Christians into our lives—friends and employers. John and I had many discussions about God and our beliefs. I believed in God, the trinity, and salvation by grace; John thought there was a God or a greater power but didn't buy much else that I believed. I did not know my Bible well enough to be able to use scripture to back up what I believed. I knew what I had been taught as a child, but I didn't know where to find supporting verses in the Bible. Besides, how do we know that what is written in the Bible comes from God? John referred to my belief as "blind faith."

John, as a university student, began to "research" the Bible to support his views. He was diligently searching for a deeper meaning and purpose in life. Although I may not have known this truth at that time, I now know with certainty that God's word is true, based on 2 Timothy 3:16 where it declares, "All scripture is inspired by God and is useful to teach us what is true and to make us realize what is wrong in our lives. It straightens us out and teaches us to do what is right." I now want to live a life based on God's leading even though it may be filled with difficulty. During my early years of marriage, this was not the path I was following.

Our first child, Jason, was born in our sixth year of marriage. Joanna followed seventeen months later. Having children brought many new dimensions to life. While they were young, I began to reflect more on God and what it means to have a relationship with Him. These reflections were not constant and were not the catalyst that led to a renewed commitment to Christ. God used his faithful servant, Pastor Billy Heath, to bring me back into a relationship with Him.

At the time, we were living in Kamloops, British Columbia, and Billy was pastoring a new church in our community. He showed up at my door, I invited him in, and we talked about God. He asked me, "Do you believe in God?" I replied, "Yes, of course I do." Billy further inquired, "I am so glad you believe. Is it fair to assume you have a relationship with Jesus? Do you frequently converse with God through prayer?" This last question caused me to hesitate, and I slowly answered, "Well, I don't pray often. I guess I only pray when I really need him. Like, after I completely mess something up and want God to fix it for me!"

We continued our conversation, and before I knew it, I was heading to church with him on Sunday. God had planned that service to be exactly what I needed to draw me back to Him. All the songs we sang were familiar to me from my childhood. The sermon summarized many of the things I had been taught as a child. I felt "at home" in this small church. Jason and Joanna both enjoyed the service and loved being with Pastor Billy. We continued to attend every Sunday. John often traveled out of town on business, but he joined us whenever he could.

Over the next couple of months, I recommitted my life to the Lord. So did John. The peace and joy I felt when I trusted in God was immense. I experienced the truth of His word, "God, who gives you hope, will keep you happy and full of peace as you believe in him. May you overflow with hope through the power of the Holy Spirit" (Rom. 5:13). Both of our children also accepted Jesus as their Lord and Savior. Jason was eight years old at the time, and Joanna was six and a half. Shortly thereafter, we were all baptized together.

CHAPTER 4

GOD ANSWERS PRAYER

O ver the next few years, my knowledge of God and my relationship with Him continued to grow. There were many answered prayers. A Christian friend once suggested that I keep a prayer journal, so I would remember all the answered prayers. She advised that it is a good practice because whenever one's faith is ebbing, it is encouraging to reflect on past experiences when God had revealed his continuous faithfulness to his followers. God is faithful to us, despite our diminishing faith. "If we are unfaithful, he remains faithful, for he cannot deny himself" (2 Tim. 2:13).

As Christians, I believe we all experience times when we have some difficulty believing God is intimately involved in our lives. At times like these, it becomes even more important to spend time drawing closer to God. Believe in His word, pay less attention to feelings, and focus more on His promises. No matter how difficult the rough patch is, God's promises stand. His word tells us to "Trust in the Lord with all your heart; do not depend on your own understanding. Seek his will in all you do, and he will direct your paths" (Prov. 3:5–6). God hears us when we seek His counsel and loves to respond to our requests. Nothing is too big for God to handle.

> Oh Sovereign Lord! You have made the heavens and earth by your great power. Nothing is too hard for you! (Jer. 32:17)

> What do you mean, "If I can?" Jesus asked. "Anything is possible if a person believes" (Mark 9:23).

Nothing is too small or insignificant to ask. He cares about all the details of our life "The steps of the godly are directed by the Lord. He delights in every detail of their lives. Though they stumble, they will not fall, for the Lord holds them by the hand" (Ps. 37: 23–24). His word tells us to "Commit *everything* you do to the Lord. Trust him, and he will help you" (Ps. 37:5).

God has answered so many of my prayers, some big and some small. Many times I am completely amazed at how He answers. I want to share some of my stories with you about the amazing ways God answers prayer. I hope you will be encouraged, even inspired, by my stories.

Within a week or so of recommitting my life to Christ, I noticed several almost immediate changes. The first had to do with the way I expressed myself. I had developed a vocabulary that included lots of words probably not found in the dictionary! As I prayed to become more like Christ, I became immediately aware that my language needed to change: "And so blessing and cursing come pouring out of the same mouth. Surely, my brothers and sisters, this is not right!" (James 3:10) I prayed for God's assistance, and He delivered. I instantaneously became sensitive to my choice of words, and eliminated the cursing with God's help. Others noticed and commented on the change in my vocabulary. This was an opportunity to give glory to God.

I was also a chain smoker, and I questioned whether this needed to change. Please note that I am not suggesting that smoking is sinful or necessary for everyone to change, but I felt that there were many reasons why I needed to quit. I had tried to quit many times in the past, unsuccessfully. Besides, I enjoyed smoking, so I was certain God wouldn't care. Maybe I should just pray about it and see if I get any clear direction from God. I began to pray, and that very night I had a dream.

The dream was that I was in church on Sunday, and a "lady of the night" attended the service that day. In my dream, she was hanging out at the back of the church in a miniskirt, painting her toenails bright red and smoking a cigarette. The cigarette was in a glitzy golden cigarette holder at least a foot long. It sparkled with jewels. I was upset that she was smoking in church. Nothing else in the dream seemed to bother me. When I awoke, I knew God had spoken to me.

Once again, I prayed for Him to help me quit smoking. I knew I could not quit on my own strength. His word promises, "For I can do everything with the help of Christ who gives me the strength I need" (Phil. 4:13). So, I tried. The first four days were horrible. I am sure I was almost impossible to live with. John didn't move out. He was patient, and I actually did quit smoking. That was twenty-five years ago, and I have not touched a cigarette since. "But with God *everything* is possible" (Matt. 19:26). This was one of the best things I have ever done for myself, and I am grateful to God for His conviction to change and His power to help me change.

In the early 1990s, while still living in Kamloops, British Columbia, we began contemplating a move back to Alberta. The employment market in Kamloops was tough; the company John had worked for had gone out of business. The economy in Edmonton was much better, and both of our families lived there. There were good reasons to make the move. However, we knew we would miss the weather, community, friends, and church family in Kamloops. We prayed for God's direction and the desire to move became stronger. The demand for housing in Kamloops, however, was not strong.

We listed our home. I was not sure that my strong desire to move to Edmonton was because it was what God wanted. Maybe it was really more what I wanted. I prayed that God would continue to guide us with the decisions we were making. I remembered a verse in the Bible that says: "And you will hear a voice say, 'this is the way; turn around and walk here'" (Isa. 30:21). I knew God would show me the way. The following morning after listing our home, John went to see our banker to find out how much the penalty would be to pay out our mortgage. I was home and praying to God to clearly show me if it was His will for us to move. I asked God to sell our house quickly if it was His will; if it was not His plan for us, not to let the house sell.

I had just finished praying when the telephone rang. It was John. He had spoken to our bank manager about the mortgage. Interestingly enough, our bank manager told him that he had a new assistant manager who would be moving from Victoria to Kamloops and needed a three-bedroom home. He thought our home would be perfect. The assistant manager was coming to Kamloops that day to look at houses. Would we be willing to show him our home that evening? Was this a coincidence? I don't think so. I knew immediately that our house would be sold, and God had answered yet another prayer. The house did sell to the assistant manager, and a month or so later, we moved to Alberta.

On our arrival in Edmonton in 1992, we stayed with John's family temporarily while we searched for a new home for our family. After much prayer, we found a lovely home that fit our budget. It had a first and second mortgage on it, which we assumed. The second mortgage was held by the realtor and had to be renewed in three months. When it became due, we could not find a bank that was willing to give us a mortgage because we were not yet well enough established in our new jobs.

The holder of the second mortgage (the realtor) threatened to foreclose. It appeared we would lose our house along with all our equity. We believed God had led us to this house. Why was this happening? We were both very anxious and upset by the situation, but also remembered God's word: "Don't worry about anything; instead, pray about everything. Tell God what you need, and thank him for all he has done" (Phil. 4:6). We prayed continually for God's deliverance.

One afternoon, John was browsing in a Christian bookstore. He was feeling stressed and searching for an answer to our dilemma. He was praying silently about this and begging God to help to avoid being foreclosed upon, when he heard an inaudible voice in his mind telling him to turn around. He did, and there was a book on the shelf right in front of his eyes entitled *God Does Not Foreclose*. The book didn't have anything to do with our situation, but John was confident that God was assuring him that He was in control. In the next few days, John received a telephone call from his brother, Chris. Chris told John that he had run into a friend whom he had not seen for thirty years. The friend had recently moved back to Edmonton and was a mortgage specialist with a bank.

Over the next few days, Chris's friend helped us obtain our mortgage. We were so thankful for the provisions of God. Shortly thereafter, the mortgage specialist moved away, and we have not seen him since. It may sound unbelievable to some, but I truly believe that God orchestrated the chain of events because of His love for us. How amazing His works are. "'My thoughts are completely different from yours,' says the Lord. 'And my ways are far beyond anything you could imagine. For just as the heavens are higher than the earth, so are my ways higher than your ways and my thoughts higher than your thoughts'" (Isa. 55:8–9).

We continued experiencing God's love in many ways over the next few years. We were growing in our faith and attending a good church. One area we had not developed was our willingness to give back to God a portion of what he gives to us. We both had satisfactory employment, but with two young children in school, money was less than plentiful. John and I agreed that if we wanted to put God first in our lives, then that should be reflected in our pocketbook. The Bible says we cannot serve two masters: "No one can serve two masters. For you will hate one and love the other, or be devoted to one and despise the other. You cannot serve both God and money" (Luke 16:13).

We decided that we would show our love and gratitude to God by faithfully tithing; we would give back to God the first ten percent of our income. We had faith that God would provide. If we give back to God what He has enabled us to earn the Lord almighty says, "I will open the windows of heaven for you. I will pour out a blessing so great you won't have enough room to take it in! Try it! Let me prove it to you!" (Mal. 3:10) I am not suggesting that we should give so God gives back more to us, but to show how faithful He is when we obey His word.

And He was faithful! The company I worked for only gave pay increases once per year in April. It was October. That very week I was given a ten percent increase. I was told it was to acknowledge my recent educational achievements. It was the first and only time this company had ever given a raise outside of the April date. To my knowledge, none have been given since. God is so faithful. His mercy and love never fails. "Trust me in your times of trouble, and I will rescue you, and you will give me glory" (Ps. 50:15).

Over the next decade many positive things happened. I completed my master's degree in business administration (MBA) and made a significant career change from the corporate world into the field of education. I taught at a local university. I love teaching and would not have changed anything about it! God has blessed me with my career. My family and I experienced excellent health and financial stability for the first time. Life was good!

There were, of course, some sad and difficult things that also happened. My mother passed away. She was eighty years old, had lived a godly life, and was ready to go and be with the Lord. One year later, one of my brothers committed suicide; he was an alcoholic and an unhappy, melancholic person. I know God is merciful and knows what is in each of our hearts. Only He knows the details of my brother's struggles and the final outcome of his life.

During this time, Jason and Joanna were young teenagers. Jason became involved in drugs, and this created many challenges. Marital conflict became the norm in our household. While John took a stricter stance with the children, I became softer. Rarely were we on the same page. We both blamed each other for the difficulties we were facing.

Focusing on our problems instead of God led to despair and unhappiness. The verse in Proverbs 4:23 "Above all else, guard your heart, for it affects everything you do" took on new meaning. Stressing over the problems and not seeking God's direction resulted in poor decision-making and a lack of wisdom on how to deal with Jason's drug addiction.

The next few years were difficult, and Jason's drug issues continued to increase. He became involved with drug-related gangs. One evening when I returned home from work, there was a message on the answering machine. I listened to it and will never forget the words I heard. A young-sounding male voice said, "If I don't get the money your son owes me, I will kill him. I will splatter his blood all over your walls. Pay attention to this warning. I am serious." The message clicked off. I was terrified. Jason was nineteen years old at the time and living at home. I knew he was extensively using drugs, and we had tried many different strategies to try to encourage him to change his behavior—to no avail.

As is common with addictions, his negative lifestyle escalated. After seeking advice from addiction experts, I believed it was time for "tough love." We needed to kick Jason out of the house.

When John came home from work, I told him about the phone message. I said, "I don't feel safe anymore, and we have more than one child to consider. We need to stop enabling Jason. We have to tell him to leave and not come back until he is off drugs." John replied, "Honey, we can't do that. How will he live? Where will he go?" I said, "I don't have those answers, but he has to go. Let's look at this as short-term pain for long-term gain." John was not in agreement, so I told him "If you are not willing to tell Jason to leave, Joanna and I will go and stay with my sister until such time as it is safe to return home." We left and within a few days, John had made Jason move out. Joanna and I returned home. I often think of this and wonder if I made the right decision.

In a matter of a week or two, Jason was in so much trouble. His life was at risk because of his gang affiliation. The problems eventually escalated to the point where Jason had to leave the city for his own safety. I will never forget the day we put him and his friend on a bus to Victoria, where they would stay with another friend. I hoped and prayed this would be a fresh start for him and an opportunity for him to turn his life around. I was to be sorely disappointed. It was only the beginning of bigger problems.

CHAPTER 5

A LIFE OF CRIME BEGINS

---◆---

When Jason first moved to Victoria, it was difficult for me to adjust to his being far away from home. He left for Victoria shortly after his nineteenth birthday in the spring of 2002. He had very little money and no job. At least he had a place to stay. We asked him to call us collect frequently, so we would know that he was OK.

He did call often, and the first few weeks we tried to help as much as we could—financially and in other ways. I sent clothes to him. I also prepared a resume and sent him copies, so he could find employment. I learned that we could offer some help, but life changes would only come about if Jason wanted to change. It didn't take long before things began to spiral downward. He was kicked out of the place he was staying and spent some time living on the streets. How do you find a job when you have no contact information?

The "friend" he had moved to British Colombia with stole all his clothes and returned to Alberta. Jason was alone and homeless! How much worse could it get? Our hope and peace must be rooted in our dependence on and trust in God. In John 16:33, Jesus said, "Here on earth you will have many trials and sorrows. But take heart, because I have overcome the world." Our trials and sorrows were many, but I reminded myself daily that God is in control. He is sovereign. This knowledge gave me the strength to persevere.

Soon thereafter, Jason met a young woman, Lindsay, and they fell in love. She was living with her mom and tried to help Jason as much as possible. He was staying with one of her friends off and on. This provided him with an opportunity to communicate with us on occasion. We were worried sick about him, and under the circumstances, it was difficult to "feel" God's promises, although we knew them to be true. I reminded myself of His promise in 2 Corinthians 4:8–9, "We are pressed on every side by troubles, but we are not crushed and broken; we are perplexed, but we don't give up and quit. We are hunted down but God never abandons us. We get knocked down, but we get up again and keep going."

I knew Jason was still involved in a drug and party lifestyle. I also knew that the people he was hanging out with in Victoria led a similar lifestyle. I felt like I had lost any control I had over his life. I needed a deeper trust in God. "Those who trust in the Lord are as secure as Mount Zion, they will not be defeated but will endure forever" (Ps. 125:1). It seemed that I no longer had any opportunities to influence Jason positively. I tried to encourage him as much as I could over the phone, although our conversations were often short and sporadic.

In mid-May of that year, John and I took a trip to Las Vegas to celebrate our twenty-fifth wedding anniversary. I spoke with Jason just before we left. He seemed troubled and sad. We had a good talk, and I reminded him that God is a loving God and one who hears our prayers. "The Lord has heard my plea. The Lord will answer my prayer" (Ps. 6:9). He was usually pretty quick to blow off any discussion about God, but this time he seemed somewhat receptive. I was encouraged and left for Vegas feeling that things were beginning to improve. That sentiment was to be very short-lived.

When we returned from Vegas, I had a call from Jason's girlfriend, Lindsay, telling me that Jason had been taken into custody and was facing charges of assault with a weapon and a home invasion. He and two other individuals had allegedly broken into the home of other criminals they knew and assaulted them. He was being held in remand. His girlfriend explained to us that he would probably be held only for a few days before being released on bail. This was not to be the case. Bail was refused, and a court date was set for October—about five months away. He would be kept at Victoria's Remand Centre until the court date.

Once Jason was able to make contact with us, he told us that his lawyer had advised him that he could possibly get somewhere between five to thirteen years imprisonment for this crime, if convicted. We couldn't believe it! Murder raps often got less than ten years! How was this possible? Apparently the British Columbia government was taking a tough stand on home invasions because there had been a significant increase in them. A home invasion was a home invasion—it made little difference if the victim was a helpless elderly couple or gang members. The details were irrelevant. I am not justifying the crime whatsoever; I just had a hard time understanding how details had no relevance.

Our feelings of helplessness obviously peaked with this new information and set of circumstances, but we continued to place our faith and trust in God. Although life was difficult and the pain kept stacking up, we knew God was in control. We believed that it might be necessary for Jason to "hit rock bottom," in order for him to be open to God's plan for his life.

June of that year was a busy month for us. Joanna graduated from high school. I wrote two MBA exams, and John and I bought a new home that would be built over the next year. The distraction was probably good for us as it helped us not to focus solely on Jason's situation. In any case, it was always there, darkening each day to some degree. We felt like our family was torn asunder; we had a gap or void that nothing could replace. It was difficult, if not impossible, to lay our burdens on God and not worry.

I knew that nothing is to be gained by worrying and that God will take care of us. "And if God cares so wonderfully for flowers that are here today and gone tomorrow, won't he more surely care for you?" (Matt. 6:30) Despite that, it seemed like I was having trouble relying on God's word. I needed to think of the bigger picture and remember that God has a plan for each of His children. It is a good plan, to prosper and not harm us—to give us a future and a hope (Jer. 29:11).

We planned a trip to Victoria for July to see Jason and reassure him of our love and support. He was able to telephone us periodically from the Remand Centre, so we did have some contact. John, Joanna, and I drove to the west coast and then took a ferry to Vancouver Island. The trip was long and exhausting. Our first visit with Jason was extremely painful. After going through security, we were led into a room where there was a glass divider separating us from our son. No physical contact was allowed. Jason was led into the room (in his orange jumpsuit), and although I had told myself I wouldn't cry, I burst into tears.

He was thin. He looked very sad, and he was so young—only nineteen years old! How could he be in such deep trouble? Our visit drew to a close much more quickly than I wanted it to. We left with a promise to return for another visit the next day. Once outside the prison, both Joanna and I cried our hearts out. A kind man approached us to see how he could help. His name was Paul. He was a Christian who had a prison ministry. We talked for a while, and he gave us some helpful information about how the visits worked. He offered to pray for us and gave us his telephone number in case we wanted to make contact with him at some point. We were grateful. After we left the prison, we went for dinner and then to our hotel room for some much-needed rest.

I was in such emotional distress that I was unable to sleep. I just wanted to die. Although I never would have committed suicide, I thought it would be a good day to get run over by a Mack truck. I could not fathom a life of visiting my young son in prison for the next thirteen years. Helplessness, hopelessness, and utter despair descended upon me. I cried out to God and prayed for most of the night. I knew that "The Lord will work out his plans for my life—for your faithful love, O Lord, endures forever. Don't abandon me for you made me" (Ps. 138:8).

The next day we were scheduled to visit Jason in the afternoon. How could I visit him and then have to leave him and travel all the way back home—fifteen hundred kilometers away? How could I leave him alone with no one to visit him? His girlfriend was under eighteen, and her father had strictly forbidden her to have any contact with Jason. As a parent, I understood this, but it hurt. He seemed so young and so alone.

After having breakfast, but before our visit, we met up with Jason's girlfriend, Lindsay, and she went with us to

Thetis Lake. She wanted to show us where she and Jason had spent time together. I still felt extremely heartsick and didn't know how I could possibly say goodbye to my son after our visit ended later that afternoon. We parked our car in a dusty parking lot and walked down to the lake. After spending about an hour at Thetis Lake, we returned to the car for our drive to the prison to visit Jason. When we arrived at our car, we noticed Paul's telephone number written in the dust on the driver's side window of our car. I asked John why and when he had written Paul's number on his window. He said, "I didn't," and on closer observation, I realized it was not his handwriting. I had not written it there, either. Neither Lindsay nor Joanna knew the telephone number. Who could have possibly written it there? Was Paul also at Thetis Lake?

When we arrived for our visit with Jason, Paul was there again, visiting another inmate. We asked him if he had put his telephone number on our window. He had no idea what we were talking about. He hadn't been to Thetis Lake, nor did he know what vehicle belonged to us. To this day, I do not know how the telephone number got there, but I definitely believe that God used someone to give me a message. God had put Paul in our path, so he could visit Jason and share God's love with him, which we were unable to do because of the distance. We were all amazed at how God had shown His mercy and provision. I felt that God had clearly shown me how much He loved me and cared for me. He had compassion for my pain and was showing me that He was in control. It was just what I needed to have the courage to return home after my visit with Jason.

Paul agreed to continue visiting Jason and to send us updates by email from time to time. I have never been more convinced of God's love for us.

And I am convinced that nothing can ever separate us from his love. Death can't, and life can't. The angels can't, and the demons can't. Our fears for today, our worries about tomorrow, and even the powers of hell can't keep God's love away. Whether we are high above the sky or in the deepest ocean, nothing in all creation will ever be able to separate us from the love of God that is revealed in Christ Jesus our Lord (Rom. 8:38–39).

We visited Jason again in Victoria in early October, shortly before his case would go to court. While waiting for the court date, we continued to earnestly pray to God for the best possible outcome.

CHAPTER 6

SENTENCING AND PRISON TIME

The court date loomed before us. With considerable anxiety, we continued to plead with God for His intervention. Although we understood that justice must be served and that God is a just God, we selfishly hoped for the shortest possible sentence.

The court date arrived in October of 2002. Due to work commitments, we were unable to travel to Victoria to attend in person. Jason's girlfriend, Lindsay, promised to be there for Jason and to let us know the outcome. She called later that evening to tell us that Jason had been sentenced to six years imprisonment. Although the sentence was lengthy, it was at the lower end of the range that his lawyer had suggested it might be. He was given some credit for time served and would be eligible for parole when two-thirds of his sentence was served. Jason would be sent from Victoria's Remand Centre to another facility in the near future.

Six years seemed like a lifetime. I was overwhelmed and wondered how I would be able to get through this extensive sentence. What would this do to Joanna and John? How would Jason get through the next six years? He portrayed a strong and intimidating exterior, but inside he had to be afraid. Jason has always been a big-hearted person, and there has never been any doubt about how much he loves his family. He needs us; we need him. We can move forward, but our family will have a hole in it for as long as he is not with us.

The correctional authorities were to determine whether he would serve his time in a medium or a maximum-security penitentiary. Once again, I prayed for God to soften the heart of his parole officer so that he would be sent to a medium security prison, rather than a maximum-security one. The parole officer, as part of the decision-making process, contacted us to do a telephone interview. During our conversation, he advised me that he was initially leaning toward sending Jason to a maximum facility, but for some reason "his heart was softened," and he had decided to recommend that he be sent to a medium security prison — Mission Institution in British Columbia's Fraser Valley. How likely do you think it is for a parole officer to use the words "softened heart" — exactly the words I had used in my prayers? Coincidence? I don't think so. God's presence and sovereignty was once again evident in the midst of our trials.

Jason was moved to the Mission Institution before Christmas of that year. Shortly after Christmas, he received a threat from another inmate. He decided that he would take action against the inmate, rather than wait for the threat to become a reality. This altercation resulted in him being transferred to a maximum-security prison in Agassiz, British Columbia — Kent Institution. The distance from our home in Edmonton to the Kent Institution was still a full day's drive. We did manage to visit him in May, a few months after his transfer. All these visits to jail were so difficult and emotionally draining. On one hand, we missed him so much and really wanted to see him, but on the other, we were filled with despair when we physically saw the toll prison life was taking on our son. Each time a visit concluded, it was so difficult to leave, not knowing when we would see him again. To this day, I remember the pain I saw in his eyes. In them was tenderness toward me, but tremendous pain as he faced his uncertain future.

In June 2003, we moved into our new home, which had taken over a year to be built. This occupied much of our focus, which was a blessing. It gave us something positive to think about. We sold the house we were living in, but we had to vacate it two weeks before we could take possession of our new home. During that two-week gap, we stayed in a hotel. Jason was unable to contact us during this time because he could only call pre-approved numbers, and the hotel line was not. He had promised to call as soon as we moved into our new home and once again had access to a telephone. Prisoners cannot receive incoming calls, nor can they call a cellular phone.

Our only methods of communicating with him were by mail or collect calls from him to a landline. I was looking forward to talking to him as soon as we moved into our new home. That phone conversation was not meant to be, which was yet another disappointment and cause for worry. About a week after moving into our new home and not having heard from Jason, I finally received a letter from him. He had been moved to the Millhaven Institution in Bath, Ontario—a maximum-security prison almost 4000 kilometers away from home.

I didn't feel like I could handle much more pain. Why had this happened? Apparently, a riot had taken place in the

Kent Institution. The rioters had started a fire, and it was believed that Jason was one of the instigators. When will he ever learn? Things seem to be going from bad to worse. How much more can we handle? I simply could not understand why God was allowing this. How could any good come out of this situation?

Later that year in October, John, Joanna, and I flew to Ontario to visit Jason. This was probably one of the most difficult visits of all. Jason was clearly struggling in this prison. It is one of the worst prisons in Canada. Most inmates had no one to visit them, and the visiting room was almost empty. The few inmates that we did see appeared to be older, bigger, and completely hardened. I felt afraid; I made sure I didn't look into their eyes. The guards watched every move we made for the complete duration of our visit.

Jason told us how he had been put into isolation or "the hole" a few times for various infractions. He further said, "I hate it here. I don't know any of the other inmates, and I don't like them, either. I have to constantly watch my back. This is a bad place—the worst of the worst!" In addition to the possible threat of harm from other inmates, there was clearly an "us versus them" mentality between the inmates and the guards. Even visitors received negative treatment from the guards. After all, if your "worthless" loved one was incarcerated, you must be worthless as well.

The environment was so oppressive, it was heart-wrenching to see. I know all things are possible for God, but how would Jason be able to survive this environment without it damaging him more? Without God there was *no* hope. Even with God, each day was a struggle. I struggled with my faith on a daily basis as time marched on.

In the spring of 2004, Jason was transferred to Edmonton Max. Although this was still a maximum-security prison, he was at least close to home, and we were able to visit him regularly, at least once a week. I was so thankful that we could see him frequently, as it was obvious that he was becoming more and more "institutionalized" and less comfortable with social interactions. I was filled with despair with the realization of how prison life was impacting Jason. Hope for the future was nothing more than a concept with no basis of reality. I sunk into a deep sea of depression.

Once the depression took hold of me, I no longer trusted God. I felt that He had abandoned my family and me. I knew and believed that nothing was impossible for Him, but He was clearly MIA — missing in action — or tending to other more important matters. I quit going to church, reading my Bible, and praying. After all, what was the point? I knew others were praying for us, and that would have to do. Maybe God would hear their prayers more than He was hearing mine.

One Sunday afternoon in the summer of that year, John and I went for a drive. Conversing in the car, I said to John, "I feel so far from God. I never hear from Him anymore. I guess that is to be expected since I never go to church, read my Bible, or pray. How can I expect Him to give me any messages?" John looked at me with a bewildered expression and responded, "Honey, don't be silly. God does not have to rely on our going to church, praying, or reading our Bible to speak to us. He can get a message to us anyway He chooses." I replied, "Yes, I suppose you are right, but He sure isn't choosing to communicate with me." The rest of our drive was an ongoing pity party on my part.

When we returned home, I had a message on my answering machine. My sister Rhoda had called, and she wanted me to call her back as soon as I could. Because I was so depressed, I didn't want to call her back and spread my negativity. Later that evening, responsibility kicked in, and I returned her call. She said, "I am so glad you called me. I have something really important to tell you. This morning when I was in church, I was praying for my boys, and I received a clear message from God. God reminded me of how you used to be so passionate about Him and always excited to go to church and share the good news of Christ with others. God told me to pray for *your* son, Jason. He assured me that he would be OK. God further told me to give you the message that Jason would be OK and that you need to resume your close relationship with Him."

I was awestruck by God's faithfulness. He had clearly given me a message through His chosen method. Rhoda's conversation with me encouraged me greatly. When I shared the afternoon conversation between John and me with her, she was also encouraged. God's word in Proverbs 12:25 came to mind: "Worry weighs a person down; an encouraging word cheers a person up." This was a turning point in my relationship with God and for the balance of Jason's prison time, I trusted in God for His strength and comfort as I waited patiently for my son's release. My heart and soul were deeply wounded, but God is a God of restoration. "He heals the brokenhearted, binding up their wounds" (Ps. 147:3).

After being at the Edmonton Max for a few months, Jason's parole officer recommended that he be transferred to the Saskatoon Correctional Centre where he would participate in an anger management program for the next year. This program would improve his chances of getting parole in 2006—two-thirds of his sentence. Jason readily agreed, and the transfer took place in the summer of 2004. Saskatoon is only about five hundred kilometers from Edmonton, so we were still able to visit Jason frequently during the year he spent there. The program seemed to be helping him.

He also seemed to be somewhat interested in and open to God. During one of our telephone conversations, in response to a comment he made about his value to God, or lack thereof, I shared a verse from Luke 12:6–7 with him. "What is the price of five sparrows? A couple of pennies? Yet God does not forget a single one of them. And the very hairs on your head are all numbered. So don't be afraid; you are more valuable to him than a whole flock of sparrows."

He didn't say too much, but a few days later during a telephone conversation with him, he said, "Mom, remember what you told me a few days ago about God caring for the sparrows? Well, after we got off the phone, I was looking out a window and I saw a couple of sparrows. I think God was showing me that he cared, and I am of value to him." I replied, "I also believe that God was speaking to you, Jason." It seemed his heart was beginning to open up to God. I was elated and thankful to God for His love, mercy, and compassion. God is so good and full of mercy. Praise His Holy name.

After completion of the one-year program, Jason was transferred from Saskatoon Correctional Centre to a medium security prison in Drumheller, Alberta. This was closer to home—less than 300 kilometers away. Because of the proximity, we were able to visit even more frequently and did so. Jason seemed to be doing better at Drumheller, partly because he had made some behavioral changes and partly because he had become accustomed to the prison environment. Hopefully, more the former and less of the latter. Another full year passed without any major incidents.

Jason's parole hearing was scheduled to determine if he would be released in October of 2006. If released, the terms would also be decided. Would he be released to a halfway house, or would he be allowed to live with John and me? We were advocating for him to be released to us, and he desperately wanted the same decision. The hearing took place, and it was decided that Jason would be allowed to return home on October 16, 2006. He had served four years—two-thirds of his six-year sentence. God had seen us through this horrific ordeal!

John, Joanna, and I traveled to Drumheller on October 15, so we could be at the prison at 8:00 A.M. the next morning to pick Jason up. We were so excited and couldn't wait to put this nightmare behind us. Of course, Jason would need to abide by the terms of his parole in order to keep his freedom. We resolved to do everything possible to influence him positively. As planned, we picked him up at 8:00 A.M. and began our drive to Edmonton. We were all so happy—especially Jason. When we stopped for breakfast en route to Edmonton, he excitedly said, "You mean I can order whatever I want for breakfast?" He couldn't believe that he had this freedom.

After we replied, "You bet," he ordered a huge breakfast and polished it off in record time. He repeatedly stated, "Wow, this is so good. I haven't had food this good for so long. Being out of prison is going to be so great! I love you guys!" I guess it is safe to assume that prison food wasn't very good! Decisions are made for inmates. They eat whatever is provided and are expected to follow orders. Life in the outside world would certainly be different. The world had changed a lot since Jason went to prison. He was now twenty-three years old. We enjoyed watching him enthusiastically embrace his freedom.

As one would expect, life was not all peaches and cream for Jason, but he seemed to be adjusting quite well to life on the outside. He soon found work and made a few friends. He was determined not to go back to jail but always feared that he wouldn't be successful. He carefully abided by the terms of his parole. I understood that Jason's success at changing life patterns would only be realized if he changed his friends. I shared my insights with him. Unfortunately, he didn't see the wisdom in my suggestion and continued to hang out with many of his old friends. Many of these friends were not strangers to crime, gangs, alcohol, and drugs. Despite the controversy over his friends, Jason adapted quite well to his new circumstances. There were a few minor setbacks, but all in all, I believed he was making good on his fresh start at a new life.

That all changed on that fateful evening in February of 2007. Jason had been arrested and charged with "accessory to murder after the fact"! While I was in Mexico traveling, my husband was home with Jason, and all was not well. One evening, Jason didn't come home. John tried to contact him all night on his cell phone, but Jason was not answering. The following morning John received a phone call from a lawyer, relating the horrific events that led to Jason's arrest. Once again, our world came crashing down!

CHAPTER 7

HERE WE GO AGAIN

As reported in the papers, Jason and three other men were caught dismembering a dead body in an apartment unit in downtown Edmonton. The police were not certain how the victim had died, but at the very least, these individuals had destroyed evidence and covered up a crime. The police immediately transported them to the police station. They were charged with "accessory to murder after the fact." The victim was a twenty-three-year-old male with extensive ties to Edmonton's drug trade. Jason never discussed the case with us, so we do not know the extent of his involvement. To date, no one has been convicted of the murder. Jason's lawyer advised him not to discuss the case with anyone, and I told him I didn't want or need to know any details. Regardless of the situation, my love for him is unconditional, and nothing can change that.

Jason was still on parole at the time of this crime. His parole was revoked, and he was quickly transferred back to the Edmonton Max. A court date was set for October 2008, and Jason would be incarcerated at the Edmonton Max until that time.

We began another stretch of time revolving around court and prison visits. I remember feeling incredibly exhausted and stressed many days. Each day, I resolved to put one foot in front of the other and do what I had to do. I reminded myself daily that God was in control and that nothing could happen without Him allowing it. He was sovereign. I tried to focus on my blessings instead of the difficulties. I was thankful that Jason was in Edmonton, and we continued to visit him weekly. We also communicated daily by telephone. Many of those conversations were difficult, but with God's strength I was able to support and encourage him.

Time in a maximum penitentiary is not meant to be easy, and it wasn't. Jason experienced and saw things that most people would never even think about. Sometimes he would be required to spend time in solitary confinement, with only his own thoughts for companionship. One time just after being released from solitary confinement, he saw one of his fellow inmates being carried out in a body bag; he had committed suicide by hanging himself in his cell. Jason also witnessed many fights, stabbings, and other serious altercations between inmates. He would often say that it was not possible to sleep without one eye open. He also said that the environment was such that one couldn't afford to be anything but aggressive. When in the jungle, one must be a lion to survive.

During this period of his incarceration, Jason was far from God. In fact, he had completely rebelled. He was investigating the Muslim faith, influenced by his Muslim cellmate. Besides, he had learned that the Muslim diet in jail provided better food! John sent Jason some material and a letter in support of the Christian faith. Jason sent a letter back to his father, venomously stating:

When I was in grade five, I believed in God. I was a born-again Christian. I believed that Jesus was my personal Lord and Savior. I bought into the idea without ever testing it—I had faith. I believed in God and felt lucky and blessed to know that God had my back and cared. I went through so much pain both at school and at home. I begged God to help me. He didn't respond. I just can't feel the words to the song "Jesus Loves Me." At this point, I stopped buying into the garbage I had been fed. I finally realize that God is a fairy tale.

Religion is a turn off. It's just a bunch of people trying to force their beliefs on others—beliefs that are not factual— belief in a paradise that you cannot prove to be real or valid. I choose to believe in nothing, except for hell on earth. I see more of the devil in mankind than I've seen God. Tell God I've been waiting for Him since grade five, and I am still waiting! This letter was very disturbing, and we continued to pray for God to draw Jason back to Him. Jason's attitude toward God remained rebellious for about a year or so, but soon returned to being somewhat neutral. He wasn't necessarily receptive to discussions about God, but his strong resistance seemed to dissipate.

Finally, in October 2008, the case was tried in court. Jason was sentenced to a four-and-a-half year prison term. Parole would not be considered until July 2011, once he served two-thirds of his sentence. He remained in the Edmonton Max until his parole eligibility date. John attended the parole hearing and spoke on Jason's behalf. Parole was denied. He was ordered to serve his full sentence that would expire in April of 2013. This was less than two years away. We encouraged him and each other. After all the time Jason had spent in prison, the final two years didn't seem unmanageable. Of course we struggled, but we mustered up the courage and strength to persevere. At least we could see a light at the end of the tunnel. We kept reassuring ourselves, knowing that once he had served his full term, he couldn't be retained any longer.

Jason's behavior was improving once again, and we were allowed to have private family visits. These were weekend visits at the prison in a private unit. We enjoyed these visits very much, and Jason really looked forward to them. Although guards frequently came to do a head count, we were mostly left alone to enjoy each other. Three years later, in October of 2011, Jason was given a transfer to a medium security prison in Grande Cache, Alberta, four hundred and thirty kilometers away from Edmonton. Although this meant our visits would be less frequent, Jason's time remaining would be easier to serve in a medium prison facility.

We continued to visit as often as we could, including several private family visits during this final stretch. Grande Cache is northwest of Edmonton. During the winter season, travel could be quite difficult. Part of the trip to Grande Cache involves traveling along a single highway that is often closed during the winter. I remember one particularly daunting voyage that took us almost twice as long as it should have. On the way to Grande Cache, the roads were excellent. We had an afternoon and evening visit with Jason. We stayed overnight in a hotel so that we could visit him again the next morning.

During the morning visit, the weather turned nasty, and we had to drive home in a snowstorm. The visibility was terrible. We could only see a couple feet in front of us. I lost track of all the vehicles we saw in the ditch along the highway. We finally made it home and were grateful that we had not been in an accident. Several times that winter, we were unable to visit Jason because of bad road conditions, but we did not lose communication with him. We heard from him almost daily by phone.

He was doing quite well at that time. He had one of the "dream" jobs at the prison in Grande Cache as the sports commissioner. This consisted of helping to plan sporting events for the inmates. He also liaised with the prison staff regarding gym equipment and other fitness-related activities. He enjoyed this work because working out and fitness was very important to him. This position gave him increased access to the gym. It helped us, knowing that he was finally able to find some happiness, despite his incarceration. Because he was finding his time behind bars a little easier, we were finding our lives a little easier also.

In early 2013, anticipation grew as the time of Jason's release was approaching. One evening in early March, I received a phone call from Jason. When I answered the phone, he was very upset. He told me "Mom, the police are going to '810' me. All the other guys in here tell me that it will probably happen." "What does that mean?" I asked. He informed me that what it means is that the police would ask a judge to restrict Jason's liberty, even though he had served his full sentence.

Under the Criminal Code of Canada, Section 810, a judge could basically force Jason to sign a contract wherein he would promise to keep the peace for a stated period of time. Other conditions would also be imposed upon him. Anyone who had reasonable grounds to fear that an individual might cause harm to himself or others, or the property of others, could request that a judge invoke this section of the statute. If the individual refused to enter into the recognizance agreement, they may be committed to prison for a period of up to twelve months. I was sure this would not happen, and I expressed my opinion to him. I said, "Jason, don't listen to all the stuff the other guys are saying. They don't necessarily know, and you all distrust the system so much, it is natural that you think this. Because of your past experiences and fears, you usually believe the worst possible situation, but that doesn't mean it will happen." I was able to calm him down somewhat because I did not think this would happen. Little did I know!

A few days later, I received a phone call from a police detective with the Edmonton Police Service's Behavioral Assessment Unit. The detective explained to me that his role was to monitor offenders who had completed their full sentences and would be living in the city but were deemed likely to reoffend, potentially causing harm to the community. He further articulated that he would be interviewing Jason in the near future to determine whether he should be placed under the supervision of his unit. I had a lengthy discussion with him, arguing against this. The detective was kind and explained that if it did happen, his objective would not be to send Jason back to jail, but to work with him to decrease the likelihood of him reoffending. Although I did not trust the system much more than my son did, I had little, if any power in the decision-making process. I really believed that it was unnecessary. I believed that Jason had learned from his experience. I believed that now that he was not doing any drugs and was actually completely against drug use, that he would not fall back into old patterns. I shared my opinion with the detective and urged him to consider my input.

John and I consulted with Jason's lawyer regarding this new turn of events. In a telephone conversation with John, she said, "John, I believe this arrangement is in Jason's best interests. I don't recommend fighting it." John responded by saying "I don't agree that this is in Jason's best interests. If he is living with us, which is the plan, we will closely watch over him and make sure he doesn't get into any more trouble." Incredulously, Jason's lawyer said, "I don't mean any disrespect, John, but wasn't Jason living with you when this whole crime cycle began?"

We couldn't argue with that. She further stated, "My opinion is that it would be very difficult for Jason to go from complete incarceration to an unsupervised environment. I can assure you that I will work on his behalf to make sure that the conditions applied to the peace bond will be reasonable. It is quite likely that the support provided by the Behavioral Assessment Unit will be beneficial to Jason's transition." We had our doubts, but we were grateful for the assistance she was willing to provide.

Later in March, the detective interviewed Jason in Grande Cache. He contacted me later to advise that although he could see that Jason had made some positive changes, he firmly believed that he would benefit from being supervised by his unit. That would be his recommendation to the court. As expected, Jason was advised shortly thereafter that he would be released under Section 810 for two years. It was expected that he would report within twenty-four hours of his release to the Behavioral Assessment Unit, and weekly thereafter. Jason was extremely agitated. He commented many times "I will never be free. This is their way of keeping me under their thumb, and they will try to throw me back in jail." I tried to encourage him, suggesting, "I understand, son, but as long as you diligently follow the terms of the agreement and work with the detectives involved, it might help you stay out of trouble. After all, what choice do you have?" Unhappily, he resigned himself to this new state of circumstances.

April 22, 2013 was Jason's release date. On April 21, he was transported from Grande Cache to Edmonton's Remand Centre. He expected to be released early the next morning. We waited the next day for the phone call telling us we could pick him up. He was not released until well into the afternoon. At long last, we picked him up and took him home. What a joyous occasion for all of us! After enjoying a nice meal together, we drove to the police station, so Jason could report to the Behavioral Assessment Unit. The detective met with our entire family. He provided Jason with a copy of the conditions and requested that they meet weekly. The detective seemed to be OK, and the terms of the agreement seemed fair and not overly onerous. Finally, his release was a reality, and his new life could begin!

CHAPTER 8

THE TRANSITION

A s a family unit, we were in agreement that Jason spend a couple of weeks at home settling into his new life before beginning the search for employment. We knew there would be many obstacles to overcome, but believed that with God's help, he would succeed. Although I knew there would be some difficulties, I guess I was naïve. I was not prepared for the heartache that was to follow. During the first week or two (the honeymoon period), the long-awaited pleasure of being together was enjoyable. We relished every moment together, trying to make up for lost time. Joanna did not live with us but had her own place, not far away. She, too, spent as much time with her brother as she could.

Jason was very fit and strong. While in prison, he had worked out in the gym daily. I realized that it was important for him to keep up with this routine. It was something positive he could do for himself. I wanted to buy him a gym pass. I suggested that he check out the local YMCA, which was close to our home. Joanna and I went with him. He was excited. The three of us went into the facility together. All of a sudden, Jason went pale and his eyes filled with stress.

He said, "I've got to get out of here. I can't do it. There are too many people," and he bolted for the door. I was momentarily stunned. I had not expected this. Joanna and I followed him outside and found him sitting on a bench, trying to calm down. We sat with him, and he explained, "I feel so panicky. It is such a big place with so many people. I am so stressed! I can't handle being around all these people." I began to realize that I had underestimated his ability to adjust to the outside world. Together we determined that we should find a smaller gym where he might be more comfortable.

We went to a small local gym in our community. When we entered, Jason approached the front desk and blurted out, "I want to find a small gym where I can work out. I was just at the YMCA but I got stressed out with all the people there. I just got released from prison." The man behind the counter was obviously shocked by Jason's disclosure. He suggested, "Why don't you try the gym out and then decide if you want to join?" While Jason worked out, I gathered pricing information from the man before I left.

Joanna stayed with Jason, and they went to her place after the workout. I hadn't been home long when I received a frantic telephone call from Joanna. She yelled, "Mom, come quick and help me. I don't know what to do. Jay lost his wallet, and he is freaking out." I began shaking and praying. I knew how frightening his panic attacks could be. Before I had a chance to leave, she called back saying "It's OK, Mom. You don't need to come. We found his wallet, and he is calm now." Although I was relieved, I felt sick to my stomach. Only out a couple of days, and here was a clear sign of extreme anxiety.

The next day we went back to the small local gym. The man who had helped us the evening before was on shift again. I said to him, "I would like to purchase a one year membership for Jason." He responded by saying "I am sorry, but the prices I gave you yesterday were incorrect. We are in the process of implementing a significant price increase, and you will have to pay the new price. I won't have the new prices for a few days, so I cannot process Jason's membership application until I have the new rates. Jason is welcome to use the facility in the interim." I left my name and phone number and requested that he call me as soon as the new prices were available. Jason continued to work out there for a couple more days and was feeling comfortable.

Two days later, I received a phone call from the man from the gym. He said, "I am sorry but some of the gym members heard Jason say he was just released from prison, and they are adamantly opposed to accepting him as a member. We need to respect the wishes of our membership and are not able to offer Jason a membership." I replied, "I am sorry to hear this. Thank you for calling." I hung up the telephone. In hindsight, I guess the price increase should have been my first clue, but it hadn't registered.

This experience made me aware that some societal members are not ready to give another human being a second chance. It would be necessary to become accustomed to this type of hurt that would probably occur more than once. Now I had to tell Jason the bad news. I was afraid he would take this rejection hard. It really upset me to give him the hurtful news. I was surprised when he took it in stride. He said he was disappointed, but we could find another gym. We did. It was bigger, but Jason adapted to it after a couple workouts. We purchased a membership for Joanna as well, and she and Jason spent lots of time together getting fit. It was a great way to bond.

It was time for the next step. It was imperative for Jason to secure employment, so he could begin earning his own money. Part of feeling "normal" involved becoming a contributing member of society. Considering Jason's criminal record and the fact that he had spent most of his adult life in jail, finding a job was not an easy task. Fortunately, the Alberta economy was robust, and lots of companies were having a difficult time filling positions. This was advantageous for Jason. John noticed online that a guy Jason had played hockey with as a young teen was the human resources recruiter for a construction company. John helped Jason reach out to him, and he agreed to interview Jason. After the interview, he hired Jason to begin work in mid-June. Another prayer answered.

Several years before Jason was released from jail, we had purchased a duplex in the west end of Edmonton, where Joanna was living. When we made the purchase, the plan was that she and her brother would be roommates at some future point. Jason was embarrassed that he was thirty years old and living with his parents. He wanted to move in with Joanna before he started his new job. He had also met a young woman through Facebook and the gym. He quickly fell in love. He wanted his own place where they could spend time together. I had hoped to have him stay with us for a little longer, but I understood his feelings. In early June, we helped him move into the family-owned duplex. He was happy to be with his sister and proud of having his own place. Much had been accomplished in six weeks. Life was beginning to look up.

In mid-June, Jason started his new job at the construction company. His first project was demolition, and he enjoyed the work. However, it soon became evident that he was having difficulty getting along with some of his coworkers. The company tried to move him to a few different job sites in an effort to find the right fit. Regardless of this, Jason soon started to miss work frequently, and he was let go. What Jason needed were some successes to build his self-esteem. Unfortunately, losing his job had the opposite result. This was coupled with relationship difficulties with his girlfriend. I never knew from one day to the next if they were broken up or together. This added to his stress. I didn't know at the time, but he had started smoking pot again. This was a violation of his release bond. Playing with fire usually leads to getting burned.

Another condition of his release was that he undergo psychological counseling. In addition to reporting weekly to the detective, he also had to report to a psychologist. He had been prescribed some anti-anxiety medication, but I was not convinced that he regularly took his medications. Once I learned that he was smoking weed, I was afraid of what the effect might be when street drugs were thrown into the mix. Maybe it wasn't only weed. All of my fears from the past began to take hold of me.

I often quoted Philippians 4:6 to myself "Don't worry about anything; instead, pray about everything. Tell God what you need, and thank him for all he has done." I released my fears to God and tried to stay positive. I tried to have an attitude of gratitude. I prayed fervently about my fears, and tried to trust God. After all, God's word says, "The earnest prayer of a righteous person has great power and wonderful results. Elijah was as human as we are, and yet when he prayed earnestly that no rain would fall, none fell for the next three and a half years!" (James 5:16b-17) My hope for Jason's future was in God's hands.

Jason needed a new job. It was summertime. My daughter and I had begun a tradition a few years prior of taking a mother/daughter vacation together every summer. This year we would be traveling to Galveston, Texas, for the first part of August. I was a little concerned about leaving Jason on his own without a job, but John assured me "Don't worry. I will watch over him and help him with his job search." While Joanna and I were in Texas, we had many phone conversations with John. He was feeling overwhelmed with all of Jason's problems. Jason had taken up smoking cigarettes again and was not focused on finding work. His relationship with his girlfriend was on-again, off-again. Each time he and his girlfriend fought, Jason would have an extreme emotional reaction. John was exhausted trying to help his son. It was during this period of time that Jason was diagnosed with Post Traumatic Stress Disorder (PTSD).

PTSD is a mental health condition often caused by a traumatic experience in which one feels helpless and fearful. Although this has been frequently observed in the military, an experience in prison may also be a cause. Emotional symptoms are depression, intense guilt, worry, and anxiety. It can also be accompanied by sleeplessness, bad dreams, and flashbacks. Jason was definitely manifesting the emotional symptoms. He was often depressed, and this affected his ability to remember and organize his tasks, much less perform them. As a child, Jason had been diagnosed with Attention Deficit Disorder (ADD). Various medications had been prescribed, but none of them seemed to work well for Jason.

As an adult, he did not want to be medicated because he felt that the drugs reduced him to a zombie state. Instead, he chose to self-medicate. Weed supposedly relaxed and calmed him. There were times his anxiety was so extreme that he could barely stand it. Despite this, he could not be convinced to go on prescribed medications. If he occasionally filled a prescription due to the urging of his psychologist, he often did not regularly take it. Many times he chose not to, but other times he simply forgot.

Shortly after Joanna and I returned from our vacation, Jason got another job at a building supply company. He was scheduled to start the first week of September. Since it had been over ten years since Jason had been on a vacation, we decided it would be good for our family to go to the mountains for the last long weekend of the summer. We cleared it with the detective Jason reported to and set off for some special family time. It was fun to watch Jason enjoy the scenic views as we traversed the mountain roads. Our destination was Kimberley, British Columbia, where we had rented a lovely resort. It had three bedrooms, a full kitchen and living room, with a hot tub on the spacious deck. We had take-out Chinese food for dinner and enjoyed a leisurely evening in the hot tub under the stars. It was idyllic. I was feeling hopeful again. Jason seemed relaxed and calm. He was relieved that he had a new job to start when we returned to Edmonton.

Once again, however, trouble reared its ugly head. Jason and his girlfriend began fighting through text messages. As it always did, their fight quickly turned toxic. It poisoned the environment and his attitude. Our weekend getaway spiraled downward. He had several full-blown anxiety attacks over the weekend, which were very difficult to witness. By the time our weekend drew to a close, we were all physically exhausted from the trip and emotionally exhausted from the drama. It was not quite the positive family experience I had envisioned and so badly wanted.

How we need God. The ongoing challenges reminded me daily of just how much. Although Jason believed God existed, he was not prepared to submit to God's will and leading in his life. We were all struggling, but God was holding us in His hands, giving us strength and comfort. Lee Strobel, in his book entitled *The Case for Faith: A Journalist Investigates the Toughest Objections to Christianity,* stated that "pain and suffering are frequently the means by which we become motivated to finally surrender to God and to seek the cure of Christ" (p. 47). I trusted God.

Perhaps these problems were necessary to draw Jason back to God. The problems also reminded me of my dependence upon God. Verse 10 of James 4 says, "When you bow down before the Lord and admit your dependence on him, he will lift you up and give your honor." There is hope in God. Jesus said, "Yes, I am the gate. Those who come in through me will be saved. Wherever they go, they will find green pastures. The thief's purpose is to kill and destroy. My purpose is to give life in all its fullness" (John 10: 9–11).

Lee Strobel also states in his book that the greatest Christians in history have often said that their sufferings ended up bringing them closer to God. This is then the best thing that could happen, not the worst (p. 47). How we frame things can be so important. Every cloud has a silver lining. We must keep our focus on God and keep praying.

After our mini family vacation, we returned to work. Jason started his new job at the building supply company. His relationship with his girlfriend was still experiencing lots of ups and downs. More downs than ups, unfortunately. Every time he had a fight with her, he became depressed and didn't go to work. He also continued self-medicating his depression. One day while he was on the job and operating some equipment, he sustained an injury to one of his fingers when the machinery crushed it. He was taken to the hospital, and his finger was stitched up. He was placed on leave with compensation for about a week while his finger healed. He mentioned to me that his boss had concerns about why the accident had happened. The best-case scenario was that he wasn't paying the necessary attention to the task. The worst-case scenario was that he was under the influence of drugs. He returned to work in early October. The first time he called in sick after that, he was terminated. Another job down the drain.

For the rest of October and into November, Jason remained unemployed. From what I understand, he continued to use drugs, including the improper use of his prescription drugs. The rocky relationship with his girlfriend continued in its on-again, off-again pattern. His relationship with his sister also began to deteriorate. She was often the recipient of his anger whenever something did not go well for him. He also had frequent outbursts of anger directed at John and me. We were all feeling frustrated with the circumstances. Joanna was feeling particularly stressed. Part of her stress was due to being the object of his frequent emotional outbursts, and part of it was a growing frustration with Jason's lack of responsibility as a roommate. Uncertainty about what to do next seemed to be the common concern of each day. What happened next removed any uncertainty we had!

On a weekday afternoon in mid-November of 2013, a crisis occurred. I had just returned home from work and was preparing dinner. John was working the afternoon shift, so he wouldn't be home for dinner. I was looking forward to a quiet evening alone. It was about 5:30 when the telephone rang. It was John, and he was frantic. He said, "Vanessa (Joanna's friend) just called me. Jason and Joanna had a huge fight. You need to go over to the house as quickly as possible. I am leaving work right now, but it will take me longer to get there."

I jumped in the car and drove to their house as fast as I could. When I arrived, Jason was in the front yard and was in a state of rage and highly agitated. We went into the house together, and I asked him what was going on. He was only minimally coherent due to his rage, but I learned that he and Joanna had a big fight and that she and her friend had taken off. Jason had punched a hole in the wall. John arrived while I was trying to learn what had happened and calm Jason down, to no avail. I was afraid he would hurt himself or inflict further damage to the house. It never crossed my mind that he might hurt me, although we were nose-to-nose yelling at each other.

When John arrived, I quietly asked him not to come in but to call the police for assistance. As he was on his cell phone to the police, Jason noticed and ran outside. He pushed his father and knocked his eyeglasses into the snow. He was yelling that he would kill himself before he would go back to jail. The police arrived, and we briefly explained what happened. They stayed to question Jason and agreed to meet us later at our home. John and I left in our car and went to find the girls. They had run from the house with no coats. Vanessa did not have any shoes on, either. Through text messaging, we were able to find them. They were freezing and hysterical. We brought them over to our house to warm up and compose themselves.

Jason had been arrested and was being taken to the police station. He still had his cell phone. While in the police car, he called me begging, "Mom, please don't send me back to jail. I promise I will try harder. I won't get so angry again. Please!" I don't remember what I said back to him—very little, I think, but I knew I had no choice. To this day, I still clearly remember that call and his voice pleading with me. It is probably a memory that will be with me forever, and it makes me feel very sad.

About half an hour later, the police arrived at our house. They needed to determine exactly what had taken place. We were asked if we wanted to press charges against Jason for the property damage. In agreement, we all opted not to press charges. Instead, I placed a call to the Behavioral Assessment Unit detective whom Jason reported to. I explained what happened. It was obvious that Jason could not live with Joanna anymore. After a lengthy discussion with the detective, he decided to have Jason sent to the Remand Centre for a couple of weeks. He would then have him placed in a halfway house. He assured me that it was not uncommon for people in these circumstances to "slip up." Perhaps some time away from his family would give Jason time to reevaluate his behavior. It was possible some good would come out of this situation.

CHAPTER 9

THE HALFWAY HOUSE

J ason spent a couple of weeks in the Remand Centre. We had telephone contact with him but no physical visitations. Of course, he regretted what had happened and wanted to live with us or Joanna upon his release. I explained to him that this was not possible. It had been decided by the Behavioral Assessment Unit that he would be placed in a halfway house. Of course he didn't want this, but there were no other alternatives. At the end of November, he was released from the Remand Centre. John and I picked him up and delivered him to the Halfway House to which he had been assigned. It was only a few blocks from where I worked. We helped him settle in, and everything seemed to be OK for a period of time. Jason had freedom during the day, and we spent lots of time together. He had resumed his relationship with his girlfriend and spent lots of time with her as well.

In early December, before Christmas, John and I took a vacation to Florida. We stayed in contact with both Jason and Joanna through text messaging. We were away for two weeks, and during that time, nothing of significance happened. When we returned, we immediately visited Jason and made arrangements with the halfway house for him to stay with us over Christmas. We were allowed to pick him up on Christmas Eve. He had to return the day after Christmas. This was his first Christmas with his family in many years. Despite the difficulties we had recently endured, we had a joyful Christmas together. I hated seeing him return to the halfway house after Christmas, but I knew that he was not yet ready to come back home.

Throughout January and into February, we continued supporting Jason as much as we could. He had a few temporary construction jobs but nothing that he stuck with. On Valentine's Day, I learned that Jason had been kicked out of the halfway house because of aggressive behavior toward staff and other residents. He would be placed in another house that had stricter rules to follow. I helped move all his belongings to the newly assigned place. He was very upset and unhappy with this turn of events. I had a heavy heart, fearing that the dark path he was on was only going to get darker. It did.

Over the next few months, it became evident that his drug usage had increased. He and his girlfriend had broken up. He had a new girlfriend who was connected to drugs and gangs. He spent more time with the new girlfriend and less time with us. We still saw him at least once a week, but most of the time, he was high. He was also manifesting extreme paranoia. Several times when I was with him, he told me that he believed his coaccuseds from his previous crime wanted to kill him.

Later, I would recall these fears. He also thought that cops were following him everywhere he went. I believed his paranoia was the root cause of these fears. The drugs he was undoubtedly taking were also a contributing factor. This behavior continued for the next several months. It was heart-wrenching for us, his family, to watch his destructive behavior. All our hopes and dreams for him had vanished. We just did not know what to do next. Once again, I found some comfort from God's word:

> When you go through deep waters and great trouble, I will be with you. When you go through the rivers of difficulty, you will not drown! When you walk through the fire of oppression, you will not be burned up; the flames will not consume you. For I am the Lord, your God, the Holy One of Israel, your Savior" (Isa. 43:2–3a).

I loved this verse so much I quickly committed it to memory. I felt like I had gone through many deep rivers, and I don't even know how to swim. On a good day, one might call it "doggy paddling." I even felt like becoming a firefighter with all the experience I had acquired fighting fires. I still love this verse and often share it with others as an encouragement to persevere. No tough patch will last forever.

John had a discussion with Jason toward the end of May 2014. Jason pleaded with John, "Dad, please let me move back home. I am not doing well at the halfway house. I need to be in a positive supportive environment in order to make the changes in my life that I need to make." John and I discussed this possibility with the detective Jason was reporting to. He agreed that it might be beneficial for Jason to return home. We all agreed that if things did not go well, Jason could be placed back at the halfway house. Jason was thrilled when we agreed to have him come back home. He willingly accepted the conditions we told him we required. He moved back home at the beginning of June.

CHAPTER 10

SECOND CHANCES

Jason's second chance to live at home started off well. He began working for a friend who owned a masonry company. He appeared to be staying off drugs. Over the summer months, he started a new full-time job, which he really liked. In August, he met a new girlfriend and started missing work, doing drugs, and violating curfew. As one would expect, this behavior resulted in him being fired once again. The new girlfriend didn't last, either. Before summer ended, they had broken up. Her influence had not been good, so we were grateful for the break-up.

He was very difficult to live with once again. John and I considered telling him he had to move out. We prayed for God's leading in our circumstances. One evening in early September, we spoke to Jason's detective to let him know what we were considering. He fully supported our decision. Before heading home, we prayed again, asking God to help us deliver the news in an appropriate way and to strengthen, protect, and guide us in our conversation. We returned home ready to tell Jason.

He met us at the door when we arrived and said, "Mom, Dad, I owe you guys a huge apology for the way I have been acting. I've been doing a lot of thinking, and I want to try harder. I know I need to try harder." He shared some of his ideas with us, which he believed would help him change. We were pretty amazed and encouraged by this unexpected change in behavior. God has promised that when we pray, things start happening. Isaiah 65:24 says, "I will answer them before they even call to me. While they are still talking to me about their needs, I will go ahead and answer their prayers!" We knew this was no coincidence, but another example of God at work.

Several days later, Jason received a call from a landscaping company he had applied to for employment. He was offered the job and started work the next day. He really enjoyed landscaping work, and he liked his boss. She recognized the areas Jason was struggling in, and seemed to know the right things to say or do to help him perform better. Her management style was what he needed to be successful. He continued to do this landscaping work until the season ended, with a promise of being rehired after the winter season. Because he enjoyed the work, he decided he would like to go to college over the winter to enroll in the landscape technician apprentice program. His boss fully supported his plan and sponsored him. He applied to Olds College and was accepted into the program, which would begin in early 2015.

Jason had a dream. One day he wanted to open his own landscaping business—a business that would be built upon the vision of employing people who needed a second chance. He would call his company "Diamond in the Rough Landscaping." John often told Jason that he was a diamond in the rough because he saw such great potential in him. Jason viewed his business as an opportunity to help others like him and to give back to society.

I have a copy of his partially completed business plan. I enjoy reading it because it reflects the real Jason, the Jason that not everyone got to see or know. Following is a quote taken from his vision and mission found in his business plan.

No one is useless. Everyone is of value. We believe in hope and rehabilitation for all. Remorse, redemption, forgiveness, and second chances can happen. No one is a throw away; no one is garbage. We believe in the underdog. We want all who were told they were not good enough and were considered a lost cause. We want the outcasts, the fallen, and the people who everyone else counted out. We want to set your hearts on fire with the flames of hope. We want to inspire all who do not believe in miracles to reconsider. We want to turn all doubters into belicvers. We care. We will make a difference. We want to see the hearts of the lost touched with compassion and newfound self-esteem. It is our mission to change the lives of as many people as we can reach. Hope is here. Every storm at some point is followed by a sunny day. Jason really cared about others, and especially people who were struggling. He was a softhearted and generous person. One day, when he and I were walking down a street in downtown Edmonton, a homeless man approached us and asked if we had a spare cigarette. Jason had four or five cigarettes left in his package. He quickly replied, "Sure, buddy. These are all I have left, but they are yours." He gave the man his cigarettes and a big smile, and we continued toward our destination. Jason was never judgmental and was always quick to give what he could to others, even when he had little himself. These were facets of his personality that I truly admired and loved.

During the fall, Jason began attending church with us more regularly. On a weekend service, he noticed that our church was offering an Alpha program on Tuesday evenings. Alpha is a program that provides some basic teaching and discussion opportunities for people who have lots of questions about faith. He decided he wanted to attend the Alpha program. He was not aware that I was involved in this ministry. When I told him I would be there because I was the class facilitator, he said, "That's great. I love spending time with my mama."

He really enjoyed the Alpha program, which ran from September to December. Every Tuesday evening he would rush into Alpha so full of enthusiasm. What he enjoyed most about Alpha were the relationships he formed with his table leaders. One of the table leaders, Dave, had a conversation with Jason just a few weeks into the program. Jason told Dave that his perception of Christians had completely changed. When he started Alpha, he expected everyone attending to judge him, especially because of his past.

He particularly expected this from the "Christians" attending. His opinion of Christians at this point in time was that they were very judgmental, unloving, unkind, and "holier than thou." He was blown away by his Alpha experience. With his usual exuberance, he shared with Dave that he felt loved, accepted for who he was, and not judged. This love is what led Jason to his next step. About halfway through the program, he recommitted his life to Christ.

On the final celebration night of the Alpha program wrap-up, in early December 2014, Jason shared with the group what Alpha had meant to him. After the evening concluded, Beulah's evangelism pastor, Angie LaFavor had a conversation with Jason. Recently, over a coffee, she shared this conversation with me. She stated, "Jason has always had a special place in my heart. Ever since I met you, many years ago, I had been praying for him. As a mother, I empathized completely with your pain and the love you felt for him. I know God's hand was in the conversation I had with Jason that night. I told him 'Jason, you have an amazing story. You need to write it down. It needs to be heard in the big room.'" Jason made light of Angie's request, but before the evening was over, she had a text from him sharing his story. Minutes later, another Beulah pastor contacted Angie and said, "Hey, do you have a great story that we could use for the Christmas Eve services?" She promptly responded, "Oh, yes. I have a great story." She could hardly believe this was happening. She knew it was no coincidence; God was at work. Jason's story of redemption would soon be shared in the big room.

Once Jason completed Alpha, he began to attend a Bible study held monthly at Dave's home. His life was on a new trajectory. John and I immediately noticed changes in Jason's attitude, demeanor, and behavior. The changes in Jason's life were manifested in many different ways. He was eager to share his love for Christ with others. He began to attend church with greater regularity and often invited friends to join him. One of his female friends frequently showed up at church with him, sometimes bringing her daughter and brother. Both she and her brother became Christians because of Jason's witness. His passion and love for God was so authentic and obvious.

John and I noticed an inner peace about Jason. His behavior became less aggressive, and he treated others with more kindness. He often expressed a desire to change his patterns—both deeds and thoughts. He was trying very hard to become a better person. Instead of reacting to situations in anger, which was his usual default, he tried to find other ways to deal with his problems. As one would expect, he continued to struggle, but there was a visible transformation in his life. Jason openly acknowledged his struggles, but he did not give up.

His favorite passages in the Bible, words that resonated with him, are Paul's words found in Romans 7:7 to 8:17. These scriptures are about how God's laws made him realize that he was a sinner. Because of his sinful nature, even though he wanted to do what was right, he just couldn't. He didn't want to do what was wrong, but he did it anyway. This propensity toward sin made him miserable. But he loved God and God's law with all his heart.

He was so grateful that because he belonged to Jesus Christ, there would be no condemnation for his sins. The Spirit had set him free; he was no longer a slave to sin. Although he continued to veer off the path he desperately tried to follow, he never lost sight of his love for God and his gratitude for all God had done for him. When comparing the recently transformed Jason with the man he had previously been, vehemently rebelling against God, it was crystal clear that God was working in his heart.

As previously mentioned, Jason's story of redemption was so unique that our church, Beulah Alliance, asked him if they could develop a video of his testimony to be shared with the congregation. Jason willingly agreed. The video was produced, and it was shown at all Beulah's Christmas Eve services, reaching thousands of people. Jason's personal witness touched many hearts. The video can be found on YouTube by searching for "Jason Costouros testimony." I am so thankful that we have this video forever. I watch it often. It comforts me and provides evidence of his salvation.

In Jason's video, he speaks frankly about his struggles. He references some things from his past that drew him away from God and led him to a life of crime. He acknowledges his brokenness and how lost he was. He had no hope. But then, he accepted Christ. He realized that God loved him and saw value in him. Life with Christ filled him with hope and peace. Because of God working in his life, he wanted to be kind to others and lift them up. These new reactions were becoming part of his personality. He ended his testimony by saying, "I owe it all to God." The changes in Jason's life expressed in this video were evident to all of us who shared life with him—both family and friends. We also owe immeasurable gratitude to God for his mercy and grace in Jason's life and in ours.

We had a late start to winter, and Jason worked well into November at his landscaping job until the season ended. John and I traveled to Thailand for a winter vacation in December. Everything was going so well for our family. While we were in Thailand, Jason reconnected with his former girlfriend. I knew there was trouble ahead. Predictably, the fighting started almost immediately. This left him angry and frustrated. Shortly after Christmas, in the midst of his relationship turmoil, he met up with a friend who had just been released from prison. They both had past addiction problems with crystal meth.

Getting together for an evening out was not a good idea. As one might foresee, the evening consisted of getting high together on this very addictive drug. Jason did not come home until the next day. In addition to the frustration and anger he was feeling as a result of his relationship troubles, he felt great remorse over using crystal meth once again. He realized he had made a terrible mistake. He told his friend that they needed to stay away from each other, so they could both try to stay away from drugs. He understood that he needed to be clear-headed to have success with his education.

After New Year's Day, we all journeyed to Olds, Alberta, to help Jason transport his belongings to the student residence at Olds College where he would be staying for the next two months. Olds is about two hours from Edmonton, so the plan was that he would travel home for weekends. I sensed that he was uncomfortable with the student residence almost immediately. He later confided in me, saying, "I feel edgy when I am at the student residence. It reminds me of being in prison." He tried to settle into this new routine, but he struggled with fitting in. If I had a dollar for every time Jason stated, "I don't know how to do life outside of prison," I would be a rich woman. He felt he didn't belong anywhere.

He continued to "talk" to his ex-girlfriend by telephone. "Fight" would be a more accurate description of his conversations with her. All of the emotional agitation led to more frequent drug use and greater unhappiness. He lost interest in his educational objective. About three weeks into the program, a situation occurred that exacerbated the downward spiral he was on.

One evening he was in his dormitory room, watching television with his door slightly open. Residents were required to keep their doors closed. Several females in another room were partying and making noise, so the residence manager came up to investigate the problem. While passing Jason's room, she slammed his door shut. This startled him. He reacted by jumping up and going into the hallway. He swore at the manager and told her, "If you ever do that again, you will be sorry. You don't know who you are dealing with." They were both very angry, and an exchange of words ensued. This happened on a Thursday evening.

Jason later told us that this particular manager didn't like him, and she was always looking for ways to irritate him. Following the altercation, Jason went downstairs and spoke with the security department. They told him that it was a rule that his door must be closed at all times. He agreed that he would be sure to do this moving forward. He apologized for his anger. It appeared that everything was handled. After classes on Friday, Jason left the campus and came home for the weekend.

We had a good weekend. He told us what had happened. We encouraged him to let it go, abide by the rules, and try to avoid that manager as best as possible. John worked with him over the weekend on some of the math that he was having difficulty with. He attended church with us on Sunday, and we enjoyed some good family time together. Jason got up very early Monday morning and drove back to Olds with a positive outlook.

He arrived on time for his first class. He felt good because he understood the computations John had helped him with. While he was in class, there was a knock on the classroom door. Two policemen had arrived. He was arrested in front of the teacher and all his classmates for threatening the residence manager. He was taken away by the police and spent the day in police custody. The detective who Jason reported to called us to let us know what had happened. He stated that he felt the charges would not stick and that he believed the situation had been blown out of proportion because of Jason's criminal record.

Despite the detective's assurances, Jason had been kicked out of Olds College and could not return. He would be allowed to pick up his belongings the following day but only with police supervision. Jason returned to Edmonton later that night. He was very distraught and humiliated. He did not want to return at all. However, he did go back the next day and picked up his personal contents. This circumstance had totally changed his future. His educational plans had gone up in smoke. He was embarrassed, discouraged, and depressed. He dreaded contacting his boss to tell her what had happened. He spent the next couple of months at home, licking his wounds. He was worried about the upcoming court case for the Old's incident. I am not sure why he made the next decision. I only know how it affected our lives.

CHAPTER 11

FORGIVENESS AND LOVE

On March 21, 2015, Jason turned thirty-two. He was registered to attend a conference with his sister and her boyfriend for the weekend. He only attended the first session of the conference and decided not to go back. He didn't like the conference because it was all about how to get rich. He thought it went against Christian principles because one of the speakers talked derogatorily about the poor. Again, this gives you a small glimpse into his soft heart for anyone he viewed as the "underdog."

On his way home from the conference, Jason got into a car accident. Someone pulled out from the right lane beside him and rear-ended him. The snow was falling, so the driver probably couldn't stop. When Jason got home, he was disturbed about the accident and the conference. He felt that disaster followed him wherever he went. He was discomfited that he was not spending his birthday with his sister. Although I prepared his favorite meal for his birthday, celebrating the occasion with his parents didn't quite "make the grade." I could see how lonely and unhappy he was. This state of depression continued to hover around him, and it seemed unshakeable.

Four days later, he did not come home in the evening. I feared something bad had happened. Early the following morning, I received a phone call from him. He was in the Remand Centre once again. The previous evening, he and a friend had been stopped by the police on suspicion of drug dealing. Although no drugs were found in the vehicle, Jason was charged with a violation of one of his conditions: being with someone with a criminal record. I don't know who he was with, but whoever it was, was known to the police. Jason was very distraught about being back in prison. I tried to assure him that everything would be OK and that we would work with his Behavioral Assessment Unit detective and a lawyer to work things out as best we could. More importantly, we would also pray. Prayer changes things.

His car had been left close to the police station in Windermere. At his request, we went and picked it up that evening and brought it back home. Jason stayed in the Remand Centre for four weeks. While in jail, he shared his faith with others. In a conversation with his father, he relayed that he had decided to get rebaptized when he got out of jail. He indicated that he knew he needed to change some of his friends and to pursue a closer walk with God.

Once released, he still had the Old's court case hanging over his head, so his future was uncertain. He was deeply troubled from this prison stint. He commented, "Not only do I not fit in the outside world, I no longer fit in prison, either." He continued to exhibit a mental state of deep discouragement.

The following week, he met with his previous boss from the landscaping company. She agreed to rehire him, but he had to complete an online course. He completed the course and resumed his landscaping work. He continued to struggle with his drug addiction and depression.

On the weekend of May 23, Jason went to a house party with a friend. His car broke down on his way home from the party, and he abandoned it. I am not sure how he got home, but the next day he seemed haunted and even more depressed. John went with him, and they were able to get the car to a garage, where it could be repaired.

Because Jason's car was being repaired, John drove him to work Monday morning. He was only at work for about an hour before he returned home. When I learned that he had blown off work again, I was furious. We had a huge argument Monday night over it. We didn't speak to each other all day Tuesday, either. I would be traveling to Atlanta, Georgia, for a conference early Thursday morning. On Wednesday morning, while getting ready for work, God placed the following verse on my heart. "And don't sin by letting anger gain control over you. Don't let the sun go down while you are still angry, for anger gives a mighty foothold to the Devil" (Eph. 4: 26–27).

I felt God telling me that I needed to make things right with Jason. He was up, also getting ready to go to work. We were still not talking to each other. I called him up to my bedroom and said to him, "Jay, I just want you to know how much I love you. My love is not dependent on what you do or don't do. I love you no matter what. I want you to understand that the reason I was so upset with you for not going to work was because I was afraid you would lose your job. I want so badly for you to transition into a normal life, and I believe that successfully holding down a job is a big part of that transition." We hugged each other. Jason said, "I know how much you love me, Mom. I never doubt that. You always have my back and I love you so much, too. Even when I get angry with you, I know you are always looking out for me." We hugged again and forgave each other. I had no idea how much God was at work in my life until a couple days later.

That Wednesday, Jason had a good day at work. He was promoted to the position of crew foreman and was thrilled about it. John was working late, so Jason and I had dinner together. I had cooked his favorite meal that night—steak and Greek salad. Over dinner, we had a great conversation about his work, promotion, and his future plans. It was reassuring to see him so happy.

Once dinner was over, I went up to my bedroom to pack for my trip. I would be leaving in the early morning hours to attend a teaching conference in Atlanta. Jason stayed home that evening because his car was still being repaired. He came to my room to talk to me while I was packing. The thought crossed my mind that he needed to discuss something serious with me. I sensed something was troubling him. When I asked what was on his mind, he said, "Nothing. I just need some Mama time." We talked, I gave him a back massage, and we had some great bonding time. I went to bed rather early, and Jason went downstairs to watch television with his dad. To this day, I believe he had something important to tell me but just couldn't bring himself to do it. He didn't like to worry me. I wish I had taken the time to encourage him to talk; it may have been key to the events that were about to unfold.

CHAPTER 12

AND THEN THERE WERE THREE

O n Thursday morning I arose at 3:00 A.M. for my travel to Atlanta. Jason woke up briefly and hugged me before I left. John drove me to the airport where I caught my flight.

On May 28, 2015, I arrived in Atlanta late in the afternoon. I texted home to let my family know I had arrived safely. Jay texted me back, telling me he loved me. I enjoyed my evening in Atlanta and went to bed around 11:00 P.M. The telephone in my room rang at about 5:00 in the morning. When I answered it, no one responded, so I went back to bed thinking someone had accidentally dialed a wrong number. A few minutes later, the phone rang again. It was the night desk manager of the hotel. He told me, "You need to call home. There had been a family emergency."

I immediately began to shake as I dialed home. There was no answer. I wondered why John hadn't called my cell phone, so I called his. He answered and asked me if I was alone. In response, I said to him, "What has happened? Who has died?" Joanna had not been feeling well when I had left, so I thought that her condition might have worsened. But deep inside, I think I knew. John answered my question. He said, "They got our boy."

Throughout the rest of the telephone conversation, I learned that Jason had been shot to death on our family home driveway at 11:22 P.M. The police had cordoned off our house, and John was with Joanna at her place. That was why he had not answered the landline. Little did I know that the wonderful evening Jason and I had shared the previous night would be the last time I would see him. The text message he sent telling me he loved me would be the last message I would ever receive from him. I still have it on my phone.

I was in deep shock and alone in Atlanta. Somehow I was able to get to the airport and rearrange all my flights so I could return to Edmonton. I traveled from Atlanta to Houston, Texas, and then to Edmonton. The plane in Houston had a problem, so we were delayed. When I boarded the alternate plane and found my seat, the first thing I noticed was a bookmark sticking out of the seat pocket. As I picked it up, I recognized the words from Psalm 23:4. "Even when I walk through the dark valley of death, I will not be afraid, for you are close beside me. Your rod and your staff protect and comfort me." In the midst of a difficult journey, this was so encouraging. It was quite the coincidence, since we were delayed partially because they had to clean the alternate plane. Despite the most heartbreaking time in my entire life, I felt some peace in my heart, knowing that God was with me and that He would walk with me in the difficult months ahead. I knew immediately that the message was not by happenstance but orchestrated by God. In the midst of my brokenness, He is strong.

John and Joanna, accompanied by my sister and broth-er-in-law, met me at the airport, and we traveled home together. During the ride home, I learned more details about Jason's murder. He had worked as scheduled that day, had dinner with his dad, and went to visit his cousin, Simone, that evening. It gives me some comfort to know that he spent his final hours on earth reading Bible stories to Simone's daughter and eating most of Simone's cookies!

Jason's car had been in the garage getting repairs all week. He had only gotten it back that day. It is believed that whoever killed him was waiting for him to return home for the evening. They knew where he lived and what vehicle he drove. When he arrived home, he was shot several times through the driver's window. He didn't even have time to turn his car lights off. Neighbors told the police they saw someone flee the scene in a pickup truck.

John heard the shots, but wasn't sure what they were. He had been in bed but not sleeping. As he went outside to see what was happening, he saw his son lying on the front seat of his car. One neighbor called the police while another tried to resuscitate Jason. He was already dead when the police and the emergency crews arrived. We were later told that he had been shot seven times. To date, his murder has not been solved. Justice has not been served. I have chosen not to be angry about this. In Lee Strobel's book, it is stated, "Justice delayed is not necessarily justice denied" (p. 45). God is a just God, and He will determine how and when justice will be served. His timing will be perfect.

My memory of the next few days is fairly hazy, most likely due to shock. Many family members and friends were at our side, bringing comfort in the best way they could. During this time, our pastor met with us to discuss funeral arrangements. He was very comforting. He shared with us that God had placed the story of Stephen on his heart as he prayed about how to comfort our family. This story is found in the book of Acts, chapter 5. As Stephen was being stoned to death, he looked up to heaven and saw God's glory, and Jesus standing in the place of honor at God's right hand. I truly believe Jason also had this experience as he was dying. He is now with the Lord forever, and we will be reunited for eternity.

The funeral took place six days later at our church. It never occurred to me that I would have to plan a funeral for my child. I had no idea what to do. I knew I wanted to honor Jason and God with whatever we did. Once I prayed, the plans fell into place. Jason spoke for himself through his video testimonial, which was played at the service. Many told us later how lovely his service was. Over three hundred people attended. Joanna eulogized her brother beautifully. She was so strong; it was evident her strength came from God.

Marilyn, a good friend of mine, had been praying with me for Jason for many years. The summer just before Jason took the Alpha program, she shared with me an impression she had received from God while praying earlier that day. As she prayed for Jason, she felt God showing her the story of Paul on the road to Damascus and relating it to Jason's life. She knew he was going to submit to God and believed that his life would make a difference for the kingdom.

Later, after Jason was killed, she was praying and asking God why this had happened. God told her that, like Paul, the scales had been removed from his eyes, and Jason could now see the light. Similar to the story of Stephen, he could now truly see God in all his glory.

Another Christian friend gave us a cross with a lovely poem on it, beautifully articulating what we believe. I would like to share the poem with you.

> Little I knew that morning, God was going
> to call your name,
> In life we loved you dearly; in death we
> do the same.
> It broke our hearts to lose you; you did
> not go alone,
> For part of me went with you the day God
> called you home.
> You left us beautiful memories; your life is
> still our guide,
> And though we cannot see you, you are
> always by our side.
> Our family chain is broken, and nothing
> seems the same,
> But as God calls us one by one, the chain
> will link again.

Another close family friend and Christian mentor to Jason shared a verse God placed on his heart and mind as he grieved Jason's passing. He believes this is what God did for Jason:

> I waited patiently for the Lord to help me,
> and he turned to me and heard my cry. He
> lifted me out of the pit of despair, out of the
> mud and the mire. He set my feet on solid
> ground and steadied me as I walked along.
> He has given me a new song to sing, a hymn
> of praise to our God. Many will see what he

has done and be astounded. They will put
their trust in the Lord (Ps. 40:1–3).

At Jason's funeral, we shared his video testimonial. As
previously mentioned, our church had produced the video
when Jason accepted Christ as his Savior. It had been shared
with the congregation the previous Christmas Eve services,
and we felt led by God to share it once again at his funeral.
Through Jason's testimony, many did see what God had
done for him, and we know of at least seven people who
have put their trust in God as a result of this—truly a difference for the Kingdom.

As for Jason, we know he is surely in a better place. God
is a merciful God and delivers us from our strife in many
different ways. He is God, and His ways and thoughts are
higher than ours (Isa. 55:9). His timing is perfect, and even
when we cannot fully comprehend His thoughts and ways,
we can trust in Him, for He is God!

CHAPTER 13

LIFE AFTER DEATH

---◆---

Two and a half years have passed since Jason's death. Our lives since his death have been difficult. We have suffered immeasurably. Have you ever awakened in the middle of the night after having a nightmare and then realized it wasn't a nightmare at all, but reality? Have you ever felt pain so excruciating that you can barely breathe? Have you ever felt a gaping hole in your heart that acknowledging its very presence brings a flood of tears to your eyes? Are you familiar with that feeling that all is not right in your world, even though you are in the midst of doing something that you typically enjoy doing?

All of these feelings have been an ever-present part of my grieving process. John, Joanna, and I all realize and understand that our lives will never be the same again. We miss Jason so much, and along with that emotion is the presence of profound sadness. Our family unit is not whole and will never be again in this life. Despite our grief, we have experienced God's presence and the truth of His words "God blesses those who mourn, for they will be comforted" (Matt. 5:4).

Death of a loved one is difficult, confusing, and heart-wrenching. Murder or suicide adds another layer of complexity. To date, Jason's murder has not been solved. Although there are many rumors about who may have committed the murder, there is no evidence. Not one single person has come forward with any viable leads. After so much time has passed, it seems reasonable to say it is a "cold case." Without resolution, there has been no closure. I know that God is a just God, and His timing will be perfect. Perhaps we are not yet ready to go through the next steps: the ordeal of a murder trial. I choose to place my trust in God, as I know He is in control and He is trustworthy.

Despite our grief, God has been faithful. Without His comfort and strength, I cannot imagine how I would have gotten through the past two years. I firmly believe that Jason has gone to be with God, and we will someday be reunited. Without this hope, I cannot imagine surviving this tragedy. I am comforted by the words in 2 Corinthians 5:6–8, "Therefore we are always confident, knowing that, while we are at home in the body, we are absent from the Lord. (For we walk by faith, not by sight.) We are confident, I say, and willing rather to be absent from the body, and to be present with the Lord." This knowledge gives me comfort. Life after death for Jason is beautiful; it is beyond our imagination.

As I have reflected on this biblical truth, I have read several books on what happens when we die. What is heaven like? Do our loved ones who have gone to be with God before us forget us? I highly recommend the following two books that have helped me a lot: *One Minute after You Die* by Erwin W. Lutzer and *Heaven* by Randy Alcorn. Christian books can be used by God to heal our broken hearts. "He is the source of every mercy and the God who comforts us. He comforts us in all our troubles so that we can comfort others. When others are troubled, we will be able to give them the same comfort God has given us" (1 Cor. 1:3b–4).

I thank God for the many ways he is bringing healing to me and my family. It is a work in progress, but I am confident that God is doing a work in me, and will continue to bring good out of a bad situation. The hopelessness one might experience when faced with the death of someone you love is often manifested in an irrecoverable state of depression. Without hope it would be impossible to overcome the intense sadness. When we place our hope in God, we can be healed. "We put our hope in the Lord. He is our help and our shield" (Ps. 33:20). I pray that justice will prevail, but I know we need to forgive Jason's murderer. John Eldredge, a Christian author, aptly explains, "Forgiveness doesn't mean it doesn't matter. It means the cross is enough" (p. 195).

I pray that Jason's life and my family's grief journey will be used for God's glory. In our weakness, He is strong. "He remembers us in our weakness. His faithful love endures forever" (Ps. 136:23). My family and I are God's children, and He loves us. We look forward to the time when God will unite our family once again and remove all our sorrows. "There will be no more death or sorrow or crying or pain. For the old world and its evils are gone forever" (Rev. 20:4).

Let me share an excerpt from Jason's Facebook page, which exemplifies his hopes and dreams. He posted this message two months before his death:

> Here I am. I am a human being. I have a soul.
> Burning like a candle. Longing to be loved .
> . . searching for truth, answers seem endless.

I have made mistakes. I will not let these mistakes dictate who it is that I become. I can change, I can grow. I can find the beauty that lingers deep beneath the pain. A thought so intriguing, yet so hard to grasp. Still I cannot let this hope face death and become the greatest of destructions. Tribulation and hardship can bloom into wisdom, growth, and peace indeed . . . I want peace, I want calm. I want to breathe like I never have before. I want to find something beautiful inside. I want to not be hardened. Letting the past be no more. Allowing myself to have faith. Letting go of my worries. Letting go of my struggles. Holding onto something new, something hopeful, something great.

Jason is now with God. His past is no more. His worries are gone forever. He is enjoying something new and something great because of his faith in the Lord. "For this world is not our home; we are looking forward to our city in heaven, which is yet to come" (Heb. 13:14).

CHAPTER 14

WORKING THINGS FOR GOOD

---◆---

"And we know that God causes everything to work together for the good for those who love God and are called according to his purpose for them" (Rom. 8:28). Many good things have happened as a result of and following Jason's death. The writing and publishing of this book is one of them. Throughout Jason's many years of incarceration, I felt God's prompting to share my journey of faith with others. I wrote several chapters, although the process was slow. On Jason's release from prison, I asked him to read what I had written. I also suggested that he write a chapter or two from his perspective. I was looking forward to a happy ending—Jason putting his past behind him and walking more closely with God. I am grateful that he had recommitted his life to God, but now he was gone. The happy ending was over. After his death, I retrieved my unfinished manuscript from his bedroom and put it away. I decided not to finish the book.

Over the next few months, several of my friends asked me how I was doing with my book. I told one of my dear friends, Carla, that I was not going to finish it because the ending was not what I had envisioned. How could his death possibly inspire anyone? She urged me to finish it. She indicated that even though the ending would be different, it could still be powerful — maybe even more so. I asked her whether this comment was her own thoughts or whether she felt led by God to encourage me. She said that it was definitely the latter.

That evening I prayed to God for His leading in writing this story. He answered my prayer through a dream. I dreamed I was a guest speaker at a large church, sharing my book with the audience. In the background, Jason's video was being shown. When I awoke the next morning, I knew I needed to finish the book. Being obedient to God had to be my first priority. He has blessed me along my journey. Writing about this tragedy has undoubtedly facilitated healing. I trust that my story will help others remain faithful to God as they experience life's rivers of difficulty.

Joanna's relationship with God grew tremendously through this tragedy. In her incredible pain, she sought God's comfort and strength. For the first time in her Christian life, she experienced the filling of the Holy Spirit in unbelievable ways. Her grief journey has culminated in a desire to help others who struggle in similar ways to her brother. In partnership with a Christian mentor and friend, she has cofounded a ministry called "Clean Break." This ministry is dedicated to helping the marginalized in society. Its particular focus is to help inmates transition from prison to life on the outside.

I have already mentioned seven people that we know of, who have accepted Jesus as their Savior because of Jason's death and testimony. It is my hope and prayer that God will use Joanna's ministry and this book to draw many others to Him. "Look! Here I stand at the door and knock. If you hear me calling and open the door, I will come in, and we will share a meal as friends" (Rev. 3:20). Jesus spoke these words. If you hear Him knocking at the door of your heart, invite Him in. "We are made right in God's sight when we trust in Jesus Christ to take away our sins. And we can all be saved in this same way, no matter who we are, or what we have done" (Rom. 3:22). If you want Jesus to be the Lord of your life, pray this simple prayer today:

> Dear Heavenly Father, I am sorry for all the things I have done wrong in my life. I accept your gift of forgiveness. I believe your son, Jesus, paid the penalty for my sins by dying on the cross. I thank you for your great sacrifice. I ask you to come into my life and make my heart more like yours. Thank you for loving me so much. In Jesus' precious name, I pray, Amen.

But to all who believed him and accepted him, he gave the right to become children of God.

—John 1:12

Let the whole earth sing to the Lord!
Each day proclaim the good news that he saves.
Publish his glorious deeds among the nations.
Tell everyone about the amazing things he does.
Great is the Lord! He is most worthy of praise!
He is to be revered above all gods.
                          — 1 Chronicles 16:23–25

Our family shortly before the life-changing
event occurred.

REFERENCES

J. Eldredge, *Moving Mountains: Praying with Passion, Confidence, and Authority.* (Nashville, Tennessee: Thomas Nelson, 2016) 195.

C. S. Lewis, *The Case for Faith: A Journalist Investigates the Toughest Objections to Christianity.* (Grand Rapids, Michigan: Zondervan, 2000) 45–47.